Little Dorrit

Dr H. M. Page was educated at King's College, Cambridge, and at Birkbeck College, London. He is now Head of the School of English and History at Newcastle Polytechnic.

Penguin Masterstudies
Advisory Editors:
Stephen Coote and Bryan Loughrey

Charles Dickens

Little Dorrit

H. M. Page

Penguin Books

Penguin Books Ltd, Harmondsworth, Middlesex, England
Viking Penguin Inc., 40 West 23rd Street, New York, New York 10010, U.S.A.
Penguin Books Australia Ltd, Ringwood, Victoria, Australia
Penguin Books Canada Limited, 2801 John Street, Markham, Ontario, Canada L3R 1B4
Penguin Books (N.Z.) Ltd, 182–190 Wairau Road, Auckland 10, New Zealand

First published 1986

Made and printed in Great Britain by
Richard Clay (The Chaucer Press) Ltd, Bungay, Suffolk
Filmset in Monophoto Times

To Jill

Contents

Note to the Reader

After a brief introduction containing preliminary suggestions about approaching the novel, this guide to *Little Dorrit* is divided into three main parts. In Part One, 'Threads', I discuss some important chapters roughly in the order in which we read them, so as to be true to our sense of the story as it unfolds, and I consider topics such as plot, characterization and themes as they appear in specific narrative moments, rather than as abstractions. As far as possible I do this from the point of view of someone reading the story for the first time. This commentary should be read with the relevant chapters of the novel; it is not intended to stand on its own. In Part Two, 'The Pattern', I go on to consider some of the major issues raised by a reading of the whole novel. Part Three, 'The Context', is concerned with *Little Dorrit*'s place in Dickens's life and literary career, and with the historical context in which it was written. Throughout the guide, I try to suggest answers to some fundamental questions: What is this novel about? How does it work? What do we need to know to understand it? How successful is it?

The weaving metaphor ('threads', 'pattern') on which the structure of the guide is based comes from Dickens's Preface to the first volume edition of *Little Dorrit* (1857). Quotations are taken from the Penguin edition, edited by John Holloway (1967, revised 1973).

Our expectations and assumptions about an author can be misleading, especially if they are unconscious and unexamined, and it can often be useful to make a brief note of what we expect and want to find in a book before we open it. This can be particularly helpful when we read Dickens, whose reputation often derives from versions of his novels adapted for the stage, cinema or television, which may differ in many ways from their originals.

Introduction: Some Clues to the Labyrinth

Little Dorrit is a long and intricate work of fiction. More than once its characters express the feeling that the world they live in is a 'labyrinth', a bewilderingly complex maze through which it is difficult or impossible to find a way. That bewilderment is sometimes shared by readers of *Little Dorrit* who find themselves lost in the entanglements of the novel. But mazes and novels are creations of the human mind, and they can be understood. What clues does Dickens offer us through the labyrinth he has created?

The first is the book's title, which directs us to its central character, the most important member of her fictional family and the moral heart of the novel. Amy Dorrit should be followed carefully, even if she is not a conventional heroine. The second clue is Dickens's division of the story into two books, 'Poverty' and 'Riches', which suggests that money, and the lack of money, are to be important, and that there is to be a contrast between the two main sections. Will there be other contrasts in the novel? The third clue is the part-issues. Dickens first published *Little Dorrit* in instalments, each containing three or four chapters (except for the last, which consisted of six chapters), deliberately designed units of narration which can be read at a sitting. The part-issues are marked with an asterisk at the ends of the appropriate chapters in the Penguin edition, and we can take advantage of these to break down our reading of this lengthy story into manageable and coherent parts. If we read an instalment every day, for example, we can complete the novel quickly enough for the story to make sense as a whole, and yet not so fast that we are bewildered by speed and unable to absorb or remember what has happened. At the end of each part we can pause and take note of how the number is designed to stand partly on its own as a narrative unit broken down in separate but related and contrasting chapters, and how it also contributes to advancing the story. If we find ourselves in a state of uncertainty or bafflement, we can at least clarify how Dickens has created it, and what we would need to know to resolve it. We also have time to note what we expect to happen, and to ponder anything else which may have occurred to us about the novel. (For a further discussion of serialization, see 'Reading on the Instalment Plan' in Part Three, pp. 116–17.)

The fourth clue is rather surprising, since it derives from a puzzling strand of the story, Arthur Clennam's attempts to find out what his dying father had meant by the mysterious message 'Do Not Forget', and to put right the injustice which he senses has been committed. Clennam spends most of the novel in a state of doubt, confusion and misunderstanding, not knowing whether a wrong has been committed, and if so, who has harmed whom and why, not being certain whether his wish to make reparation is justified or not, constantly changing his mind and constantly being misled, almost by every turn of the plot, in his determined quest for a solution to a problem he does not understand. Not until the end of the story is the secret revealed (ironically, as a result of something done by other characters) and even then the full truth is kept from Clennam. And for nearly all the novel, Dickens keeps the reader in exactly the same state of bewilderment and uncertainty as the hero. If we concentrate our attention on the confusing results of Clennam's continuing quest, then it is easy to find the plot of *Little Dorrit* unduly intricate, and difficult or impossible to remember or even summarize. One effect of Clennam's bafflement, however, is to emphasize by contrast the striking clarity of the discoveries he actually does make, even though he is not usually expecting to make them. What kind of fictional world does Clennam find when he returns home in middle age after twenty years abroad, a turning point in his life when he has to decide what to do with his remaining years? And what kind of fictional world do we find, as the narrator shows us things which Clennam does not see? It is a world full of injustices which are not mysteriously concealed in the past, but are active and visible in the present. And it is a world full of imprisonment. There are real prisons, and there are individuals and groups whose state of mind or social position feels like a prison. The best clue to *Little Dorrit* is to hold on to the thread of imprisonment until we find our way to the end of the novel and then ask whether what may have felt like a confusing labyrinth was a coherent pattern woven by Charles Dickens.

Part One: Threads

Book the First: Poverty

Sun and Shadow (ch. 1)

Few novels begin with such a fierce demonstration of an author's powers
as this. The chapter-title 'Sun and Shadow' announces the first of the
novel's subjects, and the first of its many contrasts. The first sentence is
an eleven-word paragraph which sets the time and place with cogent
brevity: 'Thirty years ago, Marseilles lay burning in the sun, one day.'
That sounds safely far away in time and space, and 'burning in the sun'
is a familiar figure of speech close to cliché. All the more surprising then
when, after a disarmingly reflective sentence which puts things in perspective by reminding us that heat is typical of southern France in
August, we are flung into a disconcerting closer look at the landscape –
or rather the landscape looks at us. In a remarkable surreal paragraph,
Dickens makes his narrator see the landscape and sky as though they
were alive, indeed human, fixedly staring at each other, and out-staring
the stranger (us). Everything in the scene – sun, houses, walls, streets,
roads, hills – stares in a universal 'staring habit', emphasized by the
repetition of the word and the repetitive patterns of the word-order,
which force the reader to stare again and again despite the intolerable
glare of light and heat Dickens evokes. From the land the narrator's
gaze moves to the sea, to the foul black harbour, polluted by humanity
(like the Thames we later see in chapter 3), which contrasts and never
mixes with the beautiful blue of the open water, and then back to the
land, to the quayside where the ships blister in the heat and the traders
of many nations and languages (listed in an order which gives no priority
to the English) seek shelter from the glare of the sea and the sky, 'set
with one great flaming jewel of fire'. Although the 'universal stare made
the eyes ache', the narrator goes on looking and experiencing, as indeed
he does throughout the book, no matter how painful or disconcerting
his perceptions are. Here we are made to feel the oppression of the heat
and light, as though plunged in 'a fiery river', and, at first, even to
welcome the contrasting darkness, damp and cold of the first of the
novel's prisons, which we seem to enter for relief and escape from forces
of nature too intense to be borne.

  Inside the prison, however, in ironical contrast, we hear an unknown
captive complain, in the first dialogue of the novel, that the sun never

shines in his cell. Dickens makes us feel that the cold and darkness are as oppressive as the blazing sun, creating a 'prison taint' by evoking the deterioration caused by enforced confinement in the polluted atmosphere of a cell which he compares to a tomb. The scene which follows gradually reveals the two main characters and the relationship between them by subtle methods which allow us, indeed require us, to notice for ourselves what is significant, and to ask questions. The narrator rarely obtrudes. We might expect there to be little scope for action in a prison, but there are two incidents, both important – food is brought to both prisoners, and one is taken off for trial on a murder charge, accompanied by howls of execration from an unseen crowd outside the prison. Our perspective is confined to the cell until the end of the chapter – a prisoner draws a map of the surrounding country on the floor of the cell, but we never escape. This helps to make us feel imprisoned.

Characters exist in relation to each other, and Dickens begins to suggest both the relationship and the differences between the two as yet unnamed prisoners when he first describes them, without comment from the narrator. The first lolls impatiently on a ledge well above the other, who is quietly lying on the stone floor (not even on the wooden bench, which we see is unoccupied). The first calls the other 'pig', and gives him a wholly unreasonable order, 'Don't sleep when I am hungry.' The second prisoner responds submissively and even cheerfully, calling the first 'master'. Their appearances contrast; the first has a small, plump, white hand, unused to manual work, and the second is tanned and looks like a working man, a sailor. The first hint of the contrasting reasons why the two men are in jail comes when the second prisoner's casual and jocular mention of the guillotine (the 'national razor') disturbs the first, who reveals his feelings, as characters so often do in Dickens, by a partly involuntary action – he 'spat suddenly on the pavement, and gurgled in his throat'. (We can guess why the throat is referred to.)

The mention of the guillotine casts a shadow over the appearance of another contrasting pair of characters, the jailer and his daughter, who come to feed the 'birds' in their cage. (This image of imprisonment, often recurring in Dickens, brings the familiar phrase 'jail-birds' to life and suggests the helplessness and vulnerability of the captives.) Father and daughter look at the birds in contrasting ways, the jailer 'sharply' (he is professionally accustomed to imprisonment and knows his captives), and the innocent child (used by Dickens, as so often, to give a new perspective on adult behaviour, to make us look afresh at the familiar) 'touched with divine compassion' for the prisoners. How should we read this? Does the child's ability to feel compassion suggest she has religious insights which her father, as an adult, has lost? Or do her feelings depend on her childish ignorance of the captives, an ignorance not shared by her father, who realizes for example that the first prisoner, who, we now learn, is called Rigaud, has deprived the second, John Baptist Cavalletto, of his fair share of food? The conflict between punishment and divine compassion becomes an important theme later in the novel when it is explicitly discussed, but here neither narrator nor characters make any comment to help us decide. It is, however, important to note how Dickens treats religion here. The child may resemble an angel in the prison, but she is a convincingly childlike figure, not a mere personification of divine pity, as we see in her intuitively natural contrasting responses to the two prisoners. She and John Baptist are happy and at ease together. She gives him his meagre food confidently, caresses his hand, and even plays a child's singing game with him. This suggests delicately Cavalletto's capacity to respond to and share the child's happy playfulness even in the prison, a gaiety which finds its natural expression in art (the singing game). Here are two paired characters who are in the prison, but not of it. In contrast, the child is afraid of Rigaud (she gives him his numerous delicacies with 'dread') and is angered by him.

The departure of the child and her father concentrates our attention on the two prisoners, on Rigaud's continuing oppressive treatment of Cavalletto (he pushes him aside with his feet) and their extremely unequal meal, ending with Rigaud's empty but meaningful gesture, gratefully received, of giving John Baptist the dregs of the wine and a cigarette. What does this oppressive and unequal relationship mean? Why does it seem natural to those involved (though not to the jailer)? The answer is given in Rigaud's assertion of his claim to be a gentleman (a position he defines by emphatically refusing to do any work, even clearing up the dominoes), a claim 'instinctively' recognized and accepted by John Baptist. This instinctive acceptance is both personal and social, partly an expression of Cavalletto's easy-going temperament and of his fear of Rigaud, and also a continuation in the prison of established convention outside. The two prisoners in their cell present us with a microcosm of the social world outside the jail in which gentlemen, who do no work, have unquestioned power over those who do work. The strength of this social system is suggested by its continuation even among prisoners. Focusing on the system at work in a concentrated form in the relations of two men in the unfamiliar context of a prison cell makes us see it more clearly. Are we to think that social relations in the wider world reproduce the relation of victimizer and victim established between Rigaud and Cavalletto in the prison? Or is this an exceptional case? At any rate, this is the first appearance in *Little Dorrit* of the theme of the gentleman and his power in society. What is a gentleman? And how does he exercise his power?

Dickens gives an interesting twist to his treatment of this theme by making Rigaud a poseur who consciously plays the role of a gentleman as though it were a game or a theatrical performance, and who imposes himself on others by determined skill in acting a part, like a confidence trickster. This makes the nature of the role as well as the skill of the performer very prominent. And by the ingenious device of facing Rigaud with an imminent trial for his life, for which he rehearses by telling his story, Dickens can make him plausibly reveal himself and his terror by a boastful and desperate attempt at self-justification intended partly to keep his spirits up and partly as practice for his role as a handsome and well-bred gentleman, with which he hopes to impose on the court and so escape punishment. His apologia, the first story within a story in *Little Dorrit*, gives us the chance to anticipate the verdict of the court, and it is easy to judge from Rigaud's version of events that he is an unreliable narrator whose wife's alleged suicide was in fact murder, committed for money. We may also be tempted to dismiss Rigaud's assertion that lawyers, politicians, intriguers and financiers all live by their wits, as he does. But, as we shall see, the world of *Little Dorrit* answers his description. Does this villain tell a truth about society, even if he lies about himself?

The action of the chapter ends with Rigaud being taken heavily guarded to his trial through a crowd convinced of his guilt which wants to tear him apart, while we are forced to stay in the cell with Cavalletto and share his unavailing wish to know what happens. At last the narrator releases us with two contrasting interventions which conclude the chapter. The first is a comparison, typical of the narrator's political radicalism, of the two criminal prisoners we have seen with 'better' captives wrongly imprisoned for reasons of state by oppressive rulers who are, in a striking metaphor, 'embalmed' after their deaths by 'polite history', servile to the powerful (as the narrator of *Little Dorrit* never is). The second intervention finally takes us out of prison back into the open air of Marseilles at sunset, now calm and peaceful. This moment of rest and relief of tension is welcome at the end of a strenuous chapter. But it is typical of Dickens that the fireflies remind the narrator of the angels, 'a better order of beings', and the calm of the sea suggests the Last

Judgment (see Revelation 20), an allusion which places the human crimes and punishments of the chapter in the context of eternity. This concludes a concentrated chapter which sets out some of the major themes of the novel, skilfully presented through the interaction of two prisoners, who we later discover play only a minor part in the rest of the story, and the jailer and his daughter, who never appear again.

Fellow Travellers (ch. 2)

This chapter begins abruptly, in the middle of a thoroughly English colloquial conversation which contrasts sharply with the stylized rendering of French idioms to which we became accustomed in 'Sun and Shadow'. There are two links with the previous chapter. One is the opening reference to 'yesterday's howling' (the noise accompanying Rigaud's departure for trial), seen now from the different perspective of someone who does not know enough to understand the incident, regarding it merely as an expression of the Marseilles character. This neatly defines time and place, while reminding us how unreliable impressions can be. The other, more important link is the fact that these respectable, well-off English travellers are also in enforced confinement (quarantined as arrivals from a plague area), at which the most prominent new character chafes and jocularly protests, calling his companions 'jail-birds'. These travellers, like the prisoners in 'Sun and Shadow', have been flung by chance into close proximity in an unfamiliar place, an arrangement which Dickens uses skilfully to reveal character and develop themes. Again, the characterization is subtle, and directions from the narrator to the reader are rare.

At the centre of the chapter is the Meagles family, the first of the family groups which are to be so important in the novel. We can call them 'middle-class' since they occupy the social space between the aristocracy and the poor. In contrast to Rigaud, the cosmopolitan, Meagles is very much an English gentleman, a successful man of business, a retired banker. He is also a complex mixture of characteristics. Does Dickens intend him to be representative and typical? Meagles is cheerful, good humoured, generous and well-meaning. He dislikes continental bureaucracy (the quarantine officials) and the unreformed English local government (beadles). He and his wife are described as 'comely', 'healthy', 'homely' and 'pleasant'. They talk of themselves as 'practical people', a phrase which in the 1850s meant hard-headed concentration on matters of business and working life to the exclusion of everything else, but which they use unconventionally by applying it to acts of spontaneous generosity and good feeling. And yet we are also led to see that Meagles has serious limitations. Although widely travelled, he insulates himself from real experience of foreign countries by refusing to learn foreign languages (like all Dickens's insular characters, he knows that foreigners understand English), and he patronizes foreigners with a good humour that does not conceal his condescension – a common attitude in Victorian England of which Dickens, who appreciated foreign ways of life, particularly those of France and Italy, strongly disapproved. More important, damaging unintentional failures of sympathy and imagination are apparent in his treatment of his fellow-travellers, and in particular of his family.

The first sign of damage we see is in the character of his daughter 'Pet', one of the three contrasting good-looking young women in quarantine. Pet, as her name suggests, has been treated as though she were still a child, cocooned in her parents' care and brought up to be lovingly dependent (an ideal of womanhood to some Victorians). The reason suggested, in a passage typical of Dickens's interest in and sympathetic understanding of the development of human character, is the effect of the death of Pet's twin sister on herself and on her elderly parents, whose grief is shown by their inability to accept the reality of the death and their need to cosset their surviving daughter. Nevertheless, however understanding Dickens may be about the causes of their behaviour, he recognizes the consequences and makes the narrator bluntly describe Pet as 'spoilt'. Her submissiveness, immaturity and lack of experience of anything but parental love make her vulnerable, a ready victim to her first persistent suitor, as we shall see.

Pet is 'paired' with her servant Tattycoram, another handsome young woman, also a victim, who has suffered the opposite fate from Pet's – her family has abandoned her and she has no parents. Mr and Mrs Meagles rescue her as a child from the Foundling Hospital with genuine compassion, although they do not adopt her but make her a servant to Pet. Dickens does not reveal Tattycoram's feelings until the end of the chapter, but they may come as no surprise if we ponder (as with Pet) the implications of Mr Meagles's naming of the child. The name given to her in the institution was 'Harriet Beadle', an 'arbitrary name', as Mr Meagles rightly says. He turns 'Harriet' into the nickname 'Tatty' and rejects the surname 'Beadle', which reminds him of local government officers. The new name imposed on the child is of course equally arbitrary: to 'Tatty' is added 'Coram', the name of the founder of the

Foundling Hospital. The result is grotesque, certain always to be noticed and inquired about (just as Clennam does), and a permanent reminder that the child has been abandoned by her parents and not adopted by Mr Meagles. The latter is entirely insensitive to this, and even thinks the 'playful' name 'might have a softening and affectionate kind of effect' on someone he expects to be bad-tempered because of her early life. It is as though Meagles has no real sense of Tattycoram's character other than that she exists to fill the role (assumed of course to be welcome to her) of servant to Pet.

Meagles's limitations are also shown in his relations with the two contrasting solitary figures, Mr Clennam and Miss Wade, who cross his path in quarantine. He is made 'very uncomfortable' by the middle-aged Clennam's description of his dreadful victimized childhood, but can make no response other than the evidently futile suggestion that Clennam should 'study and profit' from his later life, which Clennam has already described as 'always grinding in a mill I always hated'.

Miss Wade, the third handsome young woman, makes her appearance only when the travellers have been released from quarantine, taking little notice of the glare of the Marseilles sun in the 'pleasure of recovering their freedom'. This release allows Dickens to suggest the difference between liberation from quarantine (only a matter of time in this case) and inner freedom. Meagles's jocular speculation that 'a prisoner begins to relent towards his prison, after he is let out' provokes Miss Wade to insist that it is not so easy to forgive. His ludicrously cheerful reply – 'But it's not natural to bear malice, I hope?' – reveals the optimistic shallowness of his understanding of the darker human passions. He is out of his moral depth with characters such as Miss Wade, who proclaims that she would always hate and wish to destroy a place in which she had been shut up 'to pine and suffer', and leaves the others to sit alone near the 'bars of the lattice', as though choosing her own solitary confinement. Meagles is puzzled (and Pet is distressed) when Miss Wade rejects their renewed offers of sympathy and friendship and responds disconcertingly to Meagles's reminder that they may never meet again with the truism (which becomes oddly sinister in her mouth) that we are all bound to meet and interact with strangers in our lives.

The immediate consequence of this is that Dickens closes the chapter with a chance meeting (for the third time, as we later hear) between Miss Wade and Tattycoram, who is discovered alone, angrily weeping and hurting herself, furious because of her treatment by the Meagleses, full of hatred for Pet and her own subservient role. This unexpected encounter is used by Dickens to bring together these two women whose angry states of mind are similar: Miss Wade watches Tatty's emotional struggles 'as one afflicted with a diseased part might curiously watch the dissection and exposition of an analogous case', and Tatty tells Miss Wade that she seems 'to come like my own anger'. On this occasion, Tatty's conflict ends with her love for the Meagleses overcoming her hate, and she dismisses Miss Wade, leaving us with a disconcerting sense of the intensity of her fury at her position in the family.

The chapter ends with the coming of night and the dispersal of the travellers on the first of the many journeys in *Little Dorrit*. The narrator sets these in a wider perspective by comparing them to the 'restless' travels of the whole human race 'through the pilgrimage of life'. In this episode Dickens has delineated several contrasting but related characters with great economy, and so developed his central theme of imprisonment, particularly emotional limitation and confinement created and borne in different ways.

Home (ch. 3)

This remarkable chapter, the most powerful of the four in the first instalment of *Little Dorrit*, takes us 'home' to London, a prison-like city whose rain and gloom contrast sharply with the light and heat of Marseilles. It is a Sunday evening, the day of rest when work ceases, but there is no cheerful recreation for the holiday; everything is 'bolted and barred that could by possibility furnish relief to an overworked people'. Dickens assumes that we know that this oppressive restriction, on which the narrator comments with indignant irony, is caused by Sabbatarian legislation which applied the laws of the Jewish sabbath to the Christian Sunday. The question was particularly topical when *Little Dorrit* was written, since there were attempts in 1855 to strengthen the Sunday observance laws (for further details see 'Sabbatarians' in Part Three, pp. 134–5). Lack of recreation is, however, only one feature of the London of *Little Dorrit*. Through a series of disturbing images of monotony, restriction, imprisonment, misery, disease and death, the narrator creates a sense of a confined, oppressive, suffocating, melancholy and overcrowded city which threatens the life (both physical and emotional) of its inhabitants. Through the heart of the town runs a 'deadly sewer', an accurate description of the state of the Thames in the 1850s which represents the essential character of a physically and emotionally polluted city.

This is the 'home' of Arthur Clennam, to which he returns at a moment of crisis in middle life when he has decided to escape from the family business and break with his parents' belief that 'what could not be weighed, measured, and priced' (ch. 2) had no existence. Dickens makes Clennam's consciousness predominant in the chapter. For the first time in *Little Dorrit* we are given direct access to the inner life of a character, a sign of the importance Clennam is to have in the novel. His impressions of London in the present naturally stimulate recollections and re-living of the past experiences which have made him what he is, an effect typical of Dickens's interest in the working of consciousness and the development of character, and his ability to give those interests a convincing and exciting fictional form. The sound of the church-bells, as 'exasperating' to Clennam as they are 'maddening' to the narrator, starts a train of thought and feeling he cannot control and revives memories of past Sundays he has hated.

At the heart of this oppression of the young Clennam, and at the heart of the suffocating gloom of the great city, is a religious attitude (embodied in Mrs Clennam) which was very powerful in Victorian England, and which Dickens hated. He treats it as a disease of the emotions and a perversion of Christianity which causes and excuses cruelty, particularly the hateful treatment of children, inflicting 'penance in this world' and threatening 'terror in the next' (ch. 2). We can see it in Arthur Clennam's recollections of his infancy, beginning with his memory of being 'scared out of his senses' by being asked why he was going to Hell. The justification of that question was the belief that the human race is naturally wicked and depraved, and that children are inexorably bound for eternal torment in Hell unless a great and harsh effort is made to correct them. In Clennam's boyhood there follows the regimented attendance at chapel three times on a Sunday 'morally handcuffed to another boy' (more imprisonment), accompanied by deliberate under-feeding certainly not occasioned by poverty in the Clennam household. Later comes the 'interminable' Sunday of adolescence, with Mrs Clennam, 'stern of face and unrelenting of heart' reading her Bible all day. We have to wait until Clennam meets his mother again for Dickens's analysis of the emotional roots of this behaviour. As yet he simply contrasts Mrs Clennam's hard and narrow interpretation of the Bible (her copy looks as though it is ornamented by a chain, another image of imprisonment) with the true reading of the New Testament, which inspires 'sweetness of temper, natural affection, and gentle intercourse'. This is the first statement of a theme which is to be prominent in *Little Dorrit*, the contrast between different versions of the Christian religion and different readings of the Bible. One is represented by Mrs Clennam, who justifies her attachment to hatred and revenge by appealing to the harsher parts of the Old Testament, and the other by Little Dorrit, whose reliance on love and forgiveness is supported by her interpretation of the message of Christ in the New Testament. The immediate consequence of Mrs Clennam's treatment of her son is that he grows up with 'no more real knowledge of the beneficent history of the New Testament, than if he had been bred among idolators' (as in a sense he has, since Mrs Clennam's co-religionists worship their own bad passions), and he is left 'with a sullen sense of injury in his heart' – something valuable, we may reflect, since it helps him to rebel and escape.

These recollections of his childhood come to Clennam as he sits in a coffee-house wondering whether to go home to his mother's house. They are an important introduction to what follows, since Dickens uses them to summarize and review in a controlled and reflective way past experiences which become more and more disturbing to Clennam as the chapter proceeds and the past comes alive in the present. From the moment he decides to go home, his perceptions of the city darken. These descriptive paragraphs are remarkable examples of Dickens's skill in making the external world reflect and embody the feelings of his characters. Houses look like 'old places of imprisonment', and a face at a dingy window fades 'as if it had seen enough of life and had vanished out of it'. In the rain and mud Clennam goes through a deserted and decaying urban landscape which expresses his own desolation (for example, the 'wretched little bill . . . weeping on the wet wall') until he reaches the dark, miserable and precarious house of his mother, which reflects her state of mind and way of life. Here he sheds tears at the cold reception he receives from the old family servant, Flintwinch, who is reluctant even to shake hands – although this is a coldness to which Clennam is well used, never having experienced anything else at home. And yet, painful as they are, these disappointed expectations are a good sign, since they show that Clennam is still capable of 'hopeful yearnings' for something better than the life he has known.

Inside the house is the familiar furniture which calls up vivid images of punishment, cruelty and death from Clennam's memory of his experiences as a child, still alive in him and renewed in his present impression of his mother, dressed in black, sitting on a 'black bier-like sofa . . . propped up behind with one great angular bolster, like the block at a state execution in the good old days'. This sight helps to revive his earliest memories of his parents' aversion to one another and their 'rigid silence' in each other's company, a coldness re-lived in the 'glassy kiss' his mother now gives him, in the steely grey of her eyes and hair, and in her stony face. This imagery is so chilling that we can easily feel why Mrs Clennam's voice and presence renew in her son the timid reserve of his childhood. His mother talks in the intense language of the strict religionist of the 'rheumatic affection' and its 'attendant debility or nervous weakness' which have confined her to the 'prison' of her room away from times and seasons and the 'hollow vanities' of the world. But the narrator comments that she speaks of her imprisonment with 'a grim kind of luxuriousness', as though she takes pleasure in it. The same grim pleasure can be sensed in the culminating act of the encounter, her ritual evening reading of 'certain passages aloud from a book' (it must be the Old Testament), praying 'sternly, fiercely, wrathfully' that her enemies 'might be ground to dust, and that they might be utterly exterminated'. This expression of hatred revives in her son 'all the old dark horrors of his usual preparation for the sleep of an innocent child'. When he goes to his bedroom, the furniture suggests torment and suicide, and the red glare in the sky seen from his window reminds him of the hell-fire which surrounded him in youth because it was always forced upon his 'childish fancy'.

And yet, contrary to what we might expect, the chapter does not end with hell-fire, but with a very different vision as Clennam again looks out of the window and no longer sees the tormenting red glare. What has happened in between? Clennam's mood changes in another subtle paragraph which reveals Dickens's insight into the working of the mind. The news that his childhood sweetheart, from whom his mother had separated him, is now a widow and within reach is 'the last thread wanting to the pattern' of 'the web that his mind was busily weaving, in that old workshop where the loom of his youth had stood'. The other threads in the pattern are his recollection of his hopeless love for his childhood sweetheart, and his realization that Pet, the pretty girl from whom he had parted with regret in Marseilles, had attracted him because of 'some resemblance, real or imagined' to that childhood sweetheart. At this moment, in what we later see is a turning-point in Clennam's life, he begins 'to dream' again, revealing that he is not, as he had believed, incapable of hope. Dickens does not tell us what he dreams; we are left to use our imagination, like Clennam himself. Instead, the narrator comments that out of the deprivation of Clennam's gloomy life springs the wish for something better and the power to imagine what it is. The unintended result of Clennam's tormented upbringing is to stimulate

25

fancy, hope and love which can liberate him from his oppressive family. It remains to be seen whether Clennam can find will and purpose to do more than dream in a city which seems as cruelly confined as he is.

Mysteries (chs. 3–5)

The servants in the Clennam household reinforce its rigid atmosphere of gloom and repression. Jeremiah Flintwinch has a harsh name suggesting machinery ('winch') and a cold stone which gives off sparks when struck ('flint'). He even looks like the house: 'His head was awry, and he had a one-sided, crab-like way with him, as if his foundations had yielded at about the same time as those of the house, and he ought to have been propped up in a similar manner.' He also resembles Mrs Clennam in his lack of positive feelings and in the rigid tension shown in his physical appearance, his equivalent of her confinement to the wheelchair. Permanent conflict between his 'natural acerbity and energy' and 'a second nature of habitual repression' is revealed in his 'swollen and suffused' look, which, together with his twisted neck, gives him 'a weird appearance of having hanged himself at one time or another, and of having gone about ever since, halter and all, exactly as some timely hand had cut him down'. This typically Dickensian description takes an imaginative and comically horrible leap from grotesque external appearance to a sinister fantasy suggesting the violent inner life of the character. Flintwinch is also as determined as Mrs Clennam, and although he is a servant, engages in battles of will with her, standing up to her, as we shall see, on behalf of Arthur's father's reputation. She and he are two of a kind in that way, and it seems appropriate that Flintwinch should become her partner when Arthur renounces his share of the family business. On his getting the partnership, Flintwinch's eyes 'glistened as if they saw money', in contrast to Arthur's heart-felt conviction that little happiness or peace had come to the family from wealth.

Between them, Mrs Clennam and Flintwinch dominate the other servant, Affery, who is forced into marriage with Flintwinch for the sake of convenience and propriety, no more able to resist than if it had been 'a Smothering instead of a Wedding' – a comparison which neatly goes to the heart of her feelings about the way she is oppressed by her husband and her mistress. Her only resistance is vicarious – she hopes and tries to get Arthur to collide with 'the two clever ones'. Unlike Mrs Clennam, the Flintwinches are comically treated, but the humour is grotesque and black, and intensifies the grim depiction of their marriage, which, as the Clennams' had been, is devoid of love and affection – a relation of victim and oppressor.

Affery is of course excluded from the clever ones' secrets, and so Dickens can use her as an accidental and half-comprehending witness of the mysteries of the Clennam household, a device which keeps the reader uncertain. The first of her discoveries is made in the brief chapter 4 which concludes the first instalment of *Little Dorrit* when she has the first of a series of 'dreams' which recur regularly throughout the book. In this first nocturnal vision she sees her husband and his double with an iron box, of which Jeremiah is very careful. Affery notices her husband's barely suppressed violence (he lunges at his sleeping double with the candle-snuffers 'as though he would have run him through the body') and falls victim herself when he seizes her by the throat to persuade her that she has been dreaming. Dickens tells the story in such a way that although we are left in no doubt that what Mrs Flintwinch saw was 'very real in every respect', we are left wondering what it means. Who is Flintwinch's double? What is in the iron box? Why is it being sent abroad secretly on the night of Clennam's return home? Is it related to Mr Clennam's dying wish and the watchpaper which Mrs Clennam refused to discuss on the Sabbath?

No answers are given to these questions in chapter 5, 'Family Affairs', in which Clennam arranges his withdrawal from the family business and tries and fails to find out what his father's dying message meant. Had his father 'unhappily wronged any one, and made no reparation'? Has someone been 'grievously deceived, injured, ruined' because of 'grasping at money and in driving hard bargains'? The startling violence of his mother's reaction deters Clennam from asking her more questions, but there are some clues to the answers. Flintwinch insists that Arthur's father was not at fault, and hints at the real culprit: 'But your mother mentioned that you had been suspecting your father. That's not dutiful, Mr Arthur. Who will you be suspecting next?' And Mrs Clennam herself claims that her confinement 'in prison and in bonds here' for fifteen years is divinely appointed to 'make reparation' for her sins. We may well wonder whether this is related to her dying husband's message, but we are left uncertain as Clennam decides that he will get nothing more out of his mother or Flintwinch, and turns his attention to another mystery, Little Dorrit.

Dickens has so far kept Little Dorrit in the background, a barely-glimpsed figure at Clennam's first meeting with his mother, and the frightened girl who is summoned and at once dismissed to fetch Flintwinch at the second. When she comes to the foreground we see her through Clennam's eyes, a device which allows Dickens to give prominence to the workings of Clennam's mind. Little Dorrit turns out not to be a girl, but a young woman of about twenty-two whose shy behaviour and 'diminutive figure, small features and slight spare dress' give her 'all the manner and much of the appearance of a subdued child'. Like Clennam, she is quite out of place 'among the three hard elders'. But why does she disappear so mysteriously out of working hours? And why is Mrs Clennam perceptibly less harsh to her than to everyone else? Speculating on this leads Clennam to wonder whether Little Dorrit is not connected in some way with the family mysteries, and to decide to find out about her. The making of this decision is another subtly rendered example of Dickens's interest in the apparently irrational workings of the mind, and it leads us to the Marshalsea prison.

The Father of the Marshalsea (ch. 6)

Dickens concentrates chapter 6 on Mr Dorrit, touching only lightly on Little Dorrit and the rest of his family and telling the story of his many years of imprisonment, and their effect on him, with great compression and economy. The characterization is subtle, but it is done without rendering the consciousness of Mr Dorrit. This makes him, unlike Arthur Clennam, a character we look at from the outside. We do not see the fictional world through his eyes. Instead, Dickens first builds up our impression of Mr Dorrit by making the narrator describe his past and present behaviour and analyse his character and by creating another (and contrasting) character to comment on him, and then, towards the end of the chapter, leaves us to watch Mr Dorrit in action and imagine for ourselves what is going on in his mind. This is an appropriate method of characterization for a figure who, although important in the novel, is not habitually self-conscious or reflective, and whose dominant characteristics are self-deception and the wish to keep up appearances.

The chapter begins (like the book itself) 'Thirty years ago', when, we are told, the Marshalsea Prison for debtors still stood. The Marshalsea was closed in 1848, seven years before publication of *Little Dorrit* began, but imprisonment for debt was not abolished until 1869. Imprisonment for debt was a remarkably irrational and malign procedure, since it prevented the debtor from working to meet his obligations or to support himself or his family (it would only make sense in the case of a debtor who could afford to pay his creditors, but was refusing to). Dickens knew the Marshalsea well, having visited it in 1824 as a boy of twelve when his father was imprisoned there (for details, see '*Little Dorrit* and Dickens's Life', in Part Three, pp. 120–21. The fictional prison is squalid, 'close and confined', and 'hemmed in by high walls' which are 'duly spiked at top' like Clennam's bedposts (ch. 3). Inside the debtors' prison is an even more confined jail for smugglers (like Cavalletto), who had failed to pay their fines. This inner jail has by now fallen out of use because it is too confined and oppressive, although that is not officially admitted (this is the first of the pretences which pervade the official world in *Little Dorrit*).

Mr Dorrit had first been imprisoned 'long before' 1825. We first see him as he enters the Marshalsea convinced that he will shortly be released, 'a very aimiable and very helpless middle-aged gentleman', shy, irresolute, anxious, ineffectual, dependent, and effeminate in appearance. The effect of the narrator's summary of his character and description of his nervous mannerisms is reinforced by the impression Mr Dorrit makes on the turnkey, who finds himself talking to him as though he were 'a child for whose weakness he felt a compassion'. Mrs Dorrit, who hardly figures in the novel at all, is another helpless grown-up child. One of the ironies of the Dorrit family, as we later see, is that the childishness of the parents forces one of their children to take on the role of parent. Mr and Mrs Dorrit are further examples of the unsatisfactory parents so prominent in the novel (so far we have met Mr Meagles and Mrs Clennam).

Mr Dorrit's imprisonment is the result of his involvement in a partnership of which he knows no more than that he had invested money in it. The exact cause of the trouble is mysterious and incomprehensible – even the sharpest accountants are unable to sort out 'the heap of confusion'. This adds to our sense of Mr Dorrit's helplessness. (We may suppose that this financial confusion is symbolic of Mr Dorrit's state of mind, and not also a real-life possibility, but shortly after this instalment of *Little Dorrit* was published the *Saturday Review* for 9 February 1856 gave details of exactly similar 'inextricable confusion' in a real case, the Boyd bankruptcy.) Mr Dorrit is legally responsible for the debts because the action of the story takes place before the introduction of the limited liability company; at this time partners were personally liable for the business losses of partnerships and companies. The question was topical at the time of publication: limited liability was introduced in 1855 against the opposition of those who thought it immoral because it would exempt partners from taking responsibility for the consequences

29

of their actions. Given that Mr Dorrit is legally responsible, is he also morally responsible? Can he be morally responsible when he doesn't understand what has happened? Can someone who is effectively a child be held responsible? What has he done to justify imprisonment? Is he more a victim than an offender? If Dickens had made Mr Dorrit's debts simple and clear, the effect would have been to concentrate our attention on the question of the justice of imprisonment for debt. Instead, by making Mr Dorrit unable to understand what has happened Dickens raises questions about responsibility in the way proper to a novelist, primarily through fictional characters and action. The theme recurs in *Little Dorrit*, which, as we shall see, is full of characters who are irresponsible in various ways.

It is characteristic of the Dorrits, a 'poor helpless pair', that their child is unnecessarily born in prison because Mrs Dorrit leaves it too late to go to her country lodging, and that Mr Dorrit should panic so much when his wife goes into labour that he depends on the turnkey to call the doctor. For the second time in *Little Dorrit* Dickens brings a child into prison, her innocence and vulnerability helping to emphasize how revolting imprisonment is. The effect is achieved partly by the grim comedy of the birth, with the dirty doctor, who combs his hair upright by way of washing himself, and his drunken attendant looking after Mrs Dorrit in a room 'blackened with flies'.

Worse than the physical squalor, however, is the moral effect of imprisonment on the captives. The doctor, an old 'jail-bird', has found 'freedom and peace' in the Marshalsea, away from his creditors and the anxieties of the outside world, and Mr Dorrit, despite a feeble protest against having his child born in prison, begins to travel to the same point, experiencing 'a dull relief' in confinement because it keeps 'numbers of his troubles out'. The narrator comments that if Mr Dorrit had had 'strength of purpose' to 'face those troubles and fight them' he might either have escaped from prison or 'broken his heart', but instead, 'being what he was, he languidly slipped into this smooth descent, and never more took one step upward'.

The Marshalsea becomes a quiet place of refuge for Mr Dorrit, as imprisonment enters his soul and he ceases to protest against his confinement. As so often in Dickens, this state of mind is symbolized by an action – Mr Dorrit becomes such a trusted prisoner that when the jailer is ill he is often allowed to turn the key in the main gate of the prison and lock himself in. And when on the death of the turnkey he becomes the oldest inhabitant he is recognized as 'the Father of Marshalsea', a title of which he grows proud, beginning the gradual creation of an elaborate system of pretences and self-deceptions intended to dignify his imprisonment. Like Rigaud, Mr Dorrit acts the part of the gentleman and tries to impose his role on others. His pretences as Father of the Marshalsea include a tendency to exaggerate the length of his confinement and an insistence that his position should be recognized and celebrated in public ceremonies, such as the formal presentation to him of new prisoners. Mr Dorrit takes this ceremony seriously and performs it with great gravity, an effect undermined by the wits among the prisoners, who join in ironically, with 'overcharged pomp and politeness'. A similar ceremony develops for those leaving the prison, who often leave money for him anonymously in letters put under his door at night. Mr Dorrit accepts the money not as charity, but as 'tributes, from admirers, to a public character'. The donors refer jokingly to themselves as 'collegians', an old slang term ironically applied to prisoners as though they were voluntary members of a learned society. (Perhaps there is a further irony, since we do see prisoners learn in the Marshalsea – for example, the doctor and Mr Dorrit learn how to see imprisonment as a benefit, and Mr Dorrit's son Edward learns how to take the place of Mrs Bangham and become 'of the prison prisonous and of the street streety'.) Mr Dorrit is hurt if his anonymous benefactors assume facetious nicknames, since that undermines his dignity. And when these voluntary donations seem to slacken, Mr Dorrit establishes another custom, accompanying discharged prisoners to the gate, ostensibly to bid them a formal farewell as Father of the Marshalsea, but actually to apply unspoken pressure for money. When this is successful, both he and the donor conceal the gift.

What Mr Dorrit has become is shown in a short but powerful scene which ends the chapter, one of the two parallel incidents in which a poor man gives him a present he considers beneath his dignity and social position (the other is in Book Two, ch. 18). A 'Plasterer', so called to emphasize that he is a working man, not a gentleman, and that Mr Dorrit responds at first to his social status rather than his motives, gives him a parting present of halfpennies, saying, 'It ain't much, but it's well meant.' Although Mr Dorrit knows that his children have been given coins of small value which have helped to pay for his food and drink, this is the first time that he has been offered copper coins directly, and he responds angrily – 'How dare you!' and then 'feebly' bursts into tears. In response to this the Plasterer unexpectedly turns Mr Dorrit towards the wall so that others will not see his face, and this 'delicate' action

31

helps to quieten Mr Dorrit. Delicacy means acting with a proper sensitivity to the feelings of others, particularly when those feelings are painful and difficult. It is a quality much valued by Dickens, and found as often among his working men as his gentlemen. Mr Dorrit lacks it when he treats a well-meant gift as an insult. The Plasterer shows it by not taking offence at Mr Dorrit's rudeness and by responding sympathetically to his tears, which impels Mr Dorrit to acknowledge that the Plasterer's motives were kind. That recognition leads to the Plasterer offering to do more than the other ex-prisoners have ever done, to come back to visit Mr Dorrit, an offer he eagerly accepts. He is so 'downcast' afterwards that he forgets to keep up his Father of the Marshalsea role, and his fellow-prisoners notice his gloom.

This important scene is presented entirely through dialogue and incident; the narrator makes no comment on the action and gives us no direct insight into Mr Dorrit's consciousness. We are left to see for ourselves that this outbreak of genuine and spontaneous feeling, which cuts through the usual constraints of Mr Dorrit's patronizing social performance, reveals how deep in his character lies the need to keep up the pretence that he is the dignified Father of the Marshalsea who does not beg and is certainly not liable to be offered copper coins by a mere working man. And yet it also shows that he realizes that none of those who take part in his ceremonies ever come back to visit him, and that he wants genuine human feeling and affection. Does he recognize as we do that his ceremonies and class-bound attitudes stand in the way of genuine human relations, although they are an essential part of the identity he has created for himself in the prison? Or is it simply remorse at his treatment of the Plasterer that makes him 'downcast'? Dickens gives us no answer to these questions, but leaves us in no doubt how deeply imprisoned both morally and physically is the Father of the Marshalsea, who is also father (of a kind) to Little Dorrit.

The Child of the Marshalsea (chs. 7–9)

Dickens takes great care to make Amy ('Little Dorrit'), the central character of the novel, a credibly natural and complex figure. The foundation of her character is established with remarkable economy and subtlety in a few paragraphs of chapter 7. Her father and mother, as we have seen, are helpless parents who need looking after, and the child grows to meet the needs of her imprisoned family, becoming a 'Little Mother'.

Her capacity for emotional growth is not presented as an inexplicable miracle but is rendered credible by Dickens's rapid and effective presentation of the positive aspects of her environment. Because the child was born in prison she naturally attracts special attention: all new prisoners nurse her; the kind-hearted turnkey proposes himself as her godfather and becomes a substitute parent as fond of the child as she is of him, giving her what her real father can't provide. This includes both an insight into the world of work, as he buys the child an armchair which is placed in the lodge, where she can sit and watch the comings and goings of the busiest part of the prison, and an experience of leisure and freedom outside the prison, when he takes her out into the country on Sundays. He also buys her toys so that she can play. The only toy Dickens specifies is a doll, which she dresses and undresses – a game the Victorians thought natural to little girls and a reminder that Little Dorrit's role as a 'mother' is seen as a development, no doubt premature, of her natural inclinations.

Summarized in this way, the narrative may seem schematic and heavy-handed, which it is not. It is lightly done, and includes an element of astringent humour: for instance, the bachelor turnkey, however much he likes the child, nevertheless remains glad that he is not a family man himself. But Dickens has done enough to establish the child's relation with the turnkey as both natural and important, so that we can see that even in the Marshalsea and despite the deficiencies of her parents, the child enjoys care and affection and opportunities to play and learn which render her emotional development credible.

After treating the child's environment and her behaviour from the outside, Dickens goes on to render her consciousness. The innocent child's discovery of the prison is of course powerfully used as a means of making the adult reader look afresh at the full meaning of imprisonment. But Dickens also uses it to show how the environment affects the child, and how her character is influenced. The process begins with her discovery that 'it was not the habit of all the world to live locked up in narrow yards surrounded by high walls with spikes at the top'. Then she realizes that although she can go out of the prison door, she must let go of her father's hand and leave him behind. It is natural and convincing that Dickens should attribute the habitual 'pitiful and plaintive look' mixed with 'something like protection' with which she regards her father, and the 'pitiful and plaintive look' which she directs at all the inhabitants of the Marshalsea, to this discovery that her father is prevented from doing something she enjoys, and that, despite the kind-hearted turnkey's prevarications, her father is miserable in captivity, like all the prisoners.

Her consciousness is beautifully rendered in a sentence which makes use of a simply physical sensation, typical of those through which children make discoveries about their perceptions, to suggest how pervasive her sense of imprisonment is:

Wistful and wondering, she would sit in summer weather by the high fender in the lodge, looking up at the sky through the barred window, until bars of light would arise, when she turned her eyes away, between her and her friend, and she would see him through a grating, too.

The pity and protectiveness which are Little Dorrit's dominant emotions are in such ways plausibly established as the consequence of a naturally loving child growing up in a jail and responding to the sufferings of her close relative. And when the early death of her mother gives the child the opportunity to turn her look of love and pity into action, Dickens also takes care to render the change plausible by making what she does a continuation of what has gone before. She begins by leaving the livelier chair in the Lodge and sitting instead in her father's room to keep him company in earnest, a role for which her play at the turnkey's has prepared her.

Dickens's artistic tact plays an important role in the success of this portrayal of Little Dorrit as a child. The narrator concedes the limitations of his knowledge, admitting that it would be difficult to know when the child first perceived that not all the world lived in prison, guessing that Little Dorrit's pitiful and plaintive look for her father was 'perhaps' a part of her discovery that he was a prisoner, and concluding: 'What her pitiful look saw, at that early time, in her father, in her sister, in her brother, in the jail; how much, or how little of the wretched truth it pleased God to make visible to her; lies hidden with many mysteries.' This disclaimer of authorial omniscience culminates in the conclusion that 'it is enough that she was inspired to be something which was not what the rest were'. That is not artistic evasiveness but a proper, and disarming, admission of the shortcomings of human understanding. We do not fully understand how people become what they are. But before reaching those limits Dickens has described Little Dorrit's character in such a way as to establish her as convincingly human, a creature whose development is affected by her environment. She is therefore a character with secure psychological and social foundations in the world as we understand it.

The influence of Little Dorrit's environment on her character is made particularly clear when it is damaging. There is her physical size, which

Clennam comes to see as the result of years of insufficient food, and which is constantly referred to and ridiculed in the prison. It is a major obstacle to her being taken seriously, especially as a lover. As well as the shame and anxiety that results from the family's disgrace, there is her fame as the 'Child of the Marshalsea' and her consequent dislike of being pointed out to everyone and wish to conceal her birthplace and home when at work outside the prison – a concealment which increases her timidity. These psychological consequences are again not arbitrary but socially produced and convincingly rendered. They are important elements in this study of the psychological and physical influence of the environment, of what it means to be the Child of the Marshalsea.

A similar concern for credibility is found in Dickens's treatment of the consequences of Amy's tender-heartedness, established as the foundation of her character, which renders her all too liable to exploitation by those about her. This theme is early and comically introduced by the turnkey, who wants to leave his money to Little Dorrit but can't find a way of 'tying it up' so that her family can't 'come over her' and misuse it, and so dies intestate. But there is nothing funny about the way her irresponsible relatives take advantage of her heroic and selfless efforts to be a mother to her father, uncle, idle elder brother and 'wayward' sister. Little Dorrit takes charge of the family finances, arranges the education of the children (including herself) with the aid of kind-hearted prisoners who are glad to help her precisely because she is the Child of the Marshalsea, and then finds them work. She looks after her father and his helpless brother and voluntarily lives in the Marshalsea at extra expense to be close to her father. Her relatives take all this for granted as simply her duty, but they show no perception that they may have duties themselves. Clennam sees the family as 'lazily habituated to her, as they were to all the rest of their condition', viewing her 'not as having risen away from the prison atmosphere, but as pertaining to it; as being vaguely what they had a right to expect, and nothing more'.

We are left in no doubt how vulnerable Little Dorrit is to being exploited and imprisoned by her family, and how different she is from the rest of them in her response to the Marshalsea. This contrast also emphasizes how limited her effect is on her family, and how little she can change them for the better. Her father and uncle were no doubt broken men before Little Dorrit was of an age to help them, but she is also unable to influence her brother, who, despite all her efforts, appears 'to take the prison walls with him' wherever he goes, is unable to stick to any work and, at last, drawn by the 'fascination' of the Marshalsea, comes back as a prisoner like Mr Dorrit. In contrast, we see that Amy has more success outside her family, particularly with Maggy, the waif who calls her 'little mother'. Maggy is another child victim, cruelly treated by her drunken grandmother ('broomhandles and pokers'), irreparably damaged in body and mind at the age of ten by a fever, and so fixed in a permanent childhood. Nevertheless, Little Dorrit manages to help her to 'improve herself' until she is able to work and earn her own living.

Dickens also takes care to ensure that Little Dorrit is a complex character with imperfections, not a simple personification of goodness or innocence. The most important of these imperfections arises from her relationship with Mr Dorrit: she connives at the 'genteel fictions' and 'pious frauds' which are part of his role as Father of the Marshalsea. Little Dorrit is of course not habitually untruthful – the pretences are only kept up in the presence of her father and for his benefit. Clearly they breach the moral obligation to tell the truth, and they do not help William Dorrit to keep in touch with reality. Why does she do it?

The pretences arise as William Dorrit becomes more of a beggar and attempts to maintain the family gentility by refusing to acknowledge that his daughters work. Of course he knows perfectly well that they do work; what he can't tolerate is the public admission: 'With the same hand that had pocketed a collegian's half-crown half an hour ago, he would wipe away the tears that streamed over his cheeks if any reference were made to his daughters' earning their bread.' The result is that 'over and above her other daily cares, the Child of the Marshalsea had always upon her, the care of preserving the genteel fiction that they were all idle beggars together'. (Mr Dorrit's definition of gentility, we see, is the same as Monsieur Rigaud's: a gentleman must not work.)

From this wish to preserve her father from avoidable suffering derive the numerous deceits and pretences necessary to maintain the fantasy that no one in the family works. The same intention motivates Little Dorrit's concealment of her brother's imprisonment, a concealment at which all the Marshalsea connives and which only the graceless Tip himself cannot understand. Amy's determination to protect her father follows naturally from the pity and protectiveness which Dickens so convincingly establishes as the foundation of her attitude to him as a child. It is reinforced by her conviction that the Father of the Marshalsea is so irreparably damaged by his confinement that he could not survive outside the protective custody of the prison: 'How could he live?' she asks, when Clennam thinks of trying to release him.

An even more important element in Dickens's portrayal of Little Dorrit as a character with recognizable human weaknesses and imperfections is the fact that she herself is a victim of self-deceptions and delusions. Most of these delusions are about her father and are quite natural attempts to see him as better or happier than he is, or at least to find excuses for his behaviour. For example, Little Dorrit believes that the Father of the Marshalsea is 'a good, good father' because he is 'so anxious about us, you see, feeling helplessly shut up there' – an anxiety for which there is no evidence whatsoever. Similarly, she is convinced that her father is 'very much respected' in the prison because he is 'admitted to be superior to all the rest' – but we already know that Mr Dorrit is upset by the facetiousness with which prisoners play their parts in his Marshalsea ceremonies. On this delusion the narrator takes care to comment, '. . . how true the light that shed false brightness round him!', leaving us in no doubt of either the goodness of Little Dorrit's motives or the falsity of her belief. Her love is partly blind, partly deluded, and she shares to some extent the family wish not to see things as they are.

However, Little Dorrit is certainly not completely deluded. For example, we see that, whatever her illusions about her father, she is well aware that his begging is shameful and tries to stop it. Her methods are, of course, characteristically quiet; to spare her father public embarrassment she protests only silently when he begs from Clennam. Of course this appeal, though powerful in its effect on the reader, is futile, as Mr Dorrit pays no heed and Clennam gives him money. Even if we disapprove of her attitude to her father's begging, we are left in no doubt that she does not see him simply as an ideal parent. Her attitude is a mixture of contradictory feelings and perceptions, a mixture Dickens emphasizes when we first see them together, with Little Dorrit 'half admiring him and proud of him, half ashamed for him, all devoted and loving'. This complexity of feeling is not the expression of a simple delusion – Little Dorrit's love for her father does not depend on complete blindness to his faults – but it makes an important contribution to Dickens's portrayal of Little Dorrit as a natural and many-sided character, a creature of time and place.

Circumlocution (ch. 10)

We visit the Circumlocution Office, as we went to the Marshalsea prison, because of Arthur Clennam's continuing attempts to clear up the mystery surrounding his dying father's message and to make reparation for the wrong he senses has been committed. His curiosity about Little Dorrit leads him to the Marshalsea, where the intensity of his interest in the extraordinary family history of the Dorrits brings about his accidental confinement in the prison overnight. This disturbing experience provokes nightmarish speculations which include the remarkable intuitive suspicion that his mother's confinement to her room is a punishment inflicted on herself because she is responsible for Mr Dorrit's long imprisonment in the Marshalsea (ch. 8). This is another striking example of Dickens's interest in the deeper workings of the mind. We see that Clennam persists in his quest, despite all the difficulties and discouragements, because of what his upbringing has made him. He is deeply sensitive to his mother's drive to injure because he has experienced it himself, and he understands the retributive logic of her impulse to punish. His own sufferings make him sensitive to the misery of others, and he is burdened by a sense of guilt which makes him feel responsible for wrongs he has not committed and wish to make amends for them. His response to the predicament of the Dorrits is to feel pity for Amy, whose sufferings make him think of her as his 'poor child', and to try to release both Mr Dorrit and his son. Amy's belief that Mr Tite Barnacle is the most influential of the creditors detaining Mr Dorrit in the Marshalsea impels Clennam to visit the Circumlocution Office. The parade of oppressive irresponsibility he finds there contrasts sharply with Amy's assiduous care for others in the previous chapter, 'Little Mother'. There is another thematic link too with the Marshalsea chapters: the Circumlocution Office turns out to be another kind of imprisoning institution.

As in the Marshalsea chapters, Dickens introduces Arthur Clennam to experience something first described and analysed by the narrator. The Circumlocution Office is at the centre of the political system in *Little Dorrit*; it is the most important department of government, involved in all public business. It has become the most important department because of its assiduous grasp of 'the one sublime principle involving the difficult art of governing a country' – 'HOW NOT TO DO IT'. This phrase has changed its meaning since Dickens's time. It now means 'how to do something the wrong way', 'how to get it wrong'. Dickens uses it to mean 'how to avoid doing anything at all'. Professional politicians, in the view of the narrator, act on this principle in order to avoid carrying out their election promises. The Circumlocution Office goes further by applying it to all public business, making sure that no civil servant does anything useful and ensuring that all citizens who come into contact with the government are systematically obstructed.

This is achieved by creating labyrinthine administrative procedures, masses of paper and red tape, confusion, muddle and incompetence, as well as by never giving a straightforward answer to a question (hence the title 'Circumlocution Office'). If attacked in Parliament, the system is defended and 'voted immaculate, by an accommodating majority'.

The explanation of this state of affairs is given in Dickens's portrayal of the Circumlocution Office and the whole political system as a family conspiracy of the aristocracy and their hangers-on, whose sole aim is to stick tight to the power and money they can get out of the system. Dickens calls them 'Barnacles', suggesting that they are parasites who weigh down the ship of state and may in the end sink it if they are not scraped off. They use the confusion and paralysis created by the Circumlocution Office to protect their position. (The immediate historical reference here, which is to the administrative disasters of the Crimean War, is discussed in Part Three, pp. 122–31.)

The narrator's vigorously indignant description of the Office includes a brilliant satirical evocation of a Parliamentary speech, defending the indefensible. After that, by means of Clennam's futile attempt to find out the precise claims of the Office against Mr Dorrit, we are introduced to a succession of official characters, all different though all circumlocutionary. This gives comic variety to the repeated frustration of Clennam's inquiries (they all fob him off in different ways), and also helps to build up a sense of the Office as a system working through different people with a common purpose. These witty, rapidly sketched portraits are achieved partly through dialogue, of which there is a great variety ranging from casual slang to formal speech, and partly by description of external appearances, which sometimes reveal the essence of the character. Barnacle Junior is a lively caricature of the not very bright young gentleman about town. His drawled and mannered speech ('Oh, I say! Look here!') and his problems with his eye-glass (he finds it difficult to talk and keep his monocle in at the same time) comically suggest his ineptitude. In contrast Mr Wobbler and his companion are too busy at their desk spreading marmalade and polishing a gun-barrel while talking about ratting to attend to Clennam. This encounter is remarkable for the lively slang of the dialogue and the lightness with which Dickens makes his satirical point – that field sports, an obsession of the landed gentry, take precedence over public business.

Most important of all is the characterization of the head of the Circumlocution Office, Mr Tite Barnacle (the name suggests a barnacle which is particularly determined to stick). Mr Barnacle is confined to his drawing room by an attack of that eminently aristocratic disease, gout, and this allows Dickens to bring his house into the story in such a way as to represent his social position and moral character. The house, one of a number of 'abject hangers-on to a fashionable situation', not quite in Grosvenor Square, is small, airless and confined, though of course very expensive. The comic treatment of Clennam's entrance to the house, particularly his farcical encounter with the footman in the narrow passage, serves both to undermine the absurdly pretentious dignity of the establishment and to add to the impressions of confinement we receive when he is 'shut up' in a small room looking out at 'a low blinding wall three feet off'. Further suggestions of imprisonment are found in the 'altogether splendid, massive, overpowering, and impracticable' figure of Mr Tite Barnacle himself, with his leg on a rest. His stiff, old-fashioned dress and manner are as inconvenient and oppressive as his house, and represent his circumlocutionary activities: 'He wound and wound folds of white cravat round his neck, as he wound and wound folds of tape and paper round the neck of the country.' (This sinister image, with its suggestions of strangulation, recalls the image of suicide by hanging which Dickens used to characterize another restricted and restricting figure, Mr Flintwinch.) By contrast, the last member of the Barnacle family is the lively and affable young aristocrat who knows perfectly well that the Circumlocution Office is 'a piece of machinery' for maintaining aristocratic privilege, and who brings Clennam's wasted day in the department to an end by outlining the hopelessly convoluted procedure he will have to follow to find out about Mr Dorrit, giving him 'lots of forms' and recommending him 'not to bother himself'.

Dickens now reinforces Clennam's experience of Circumlocution by introducing a new character, Daniel Doyce. As he leaves the Office, Clennam unexpectedly meets Mr Meagles, last seen in Marseilles. He seems to be angry with a stranger, whom he treats like 'a public offender'. It turns out that the stranger is Doyce, and Mr Meagles's anger is really directed at the Circumlocution officials, whose attitude to Doyce he satirizes by imitation. Doyce is an engineer and the inventor of a process (left undefined by Dickens so as not to divert our attention with details) which would be of great public benefit if adopted by the government. Doyce has been left older, sterner and poorer because of his long and futile attempts to persuade the Circumlocution Office of the value of his invention, which is, however, recognized and exploited abroad. Dickens characterizes Doyce by his thoughtful face, 'quiet, deliberate manner', and gestures which suggest his practical ability – for example, 'a certain free use of the thumb that is never seen but in a hand accustomed to tools'. Of course, none of this impresses the 'highly connected gentlemen' of the Circumlocution Office, who discourage, ill-treat and thwart all those with 'projects for the general welfare'. (For a real-life case of this, see 'Barnacles and Benefactors' in Part Three, pp. 133–4.) With this example of 'How not to do it' stifling the inventive powers of a potential public benefactor, Dickens concludes a highly compressed and lively chapter which introduces the central political institution in *Little Dorrit*, the Circumlocution Office, an organization for confining and paralysing the country, and strangling it in red tape.

Bleeding Heart Yard (chs. 12, 13 and others)

Bleeding Heart Yard is a former aristocratic mansion now subdivided and inhabited by poor people who live among its 'faded glories'. Dickens alerts us to the implications of its name at the end of chapter 10, when Clennam reflects that 'Bleeding Heart Yard was no inappropriate destination for a man who had been in official correspondence with my lords and the Barnacles', and perhaps also, according to the narrator, has a misgiving 'that Britannia herself might come to look for lodgings in Bleeding Heart Yard, some ugly day or other, if she over-did the Circumlocution Office'. These suggestions of unhappiness and misfortune are confirmed when we see Bleeding Heart Yard, which turns out to be another kind of prison full of victims of poverty and oppression, representing the miserable life of the poor in Victorian England.

We enter the Yard with Arthur Clennam, who has gone there to arrange Tip's release from the Marshalsea. To this end he visits the home of Mr Plornish, the plasterer who gave the halfpennies to Mr Dorrit. There is a subtle but striking incident when Clennam enters the house and removes his hat without thinking – a courtesy which he takes for granted, but which Mrs Plornish tells us is unusual: 'It ain't many that comes into a poor place, that deems it worth their while to move their hats.' This reminds us sharply that class distinctions are taken to justify rudeness and lack of respect by the rich to the poor. Clennam, characteristically, treats Mrs Plornish with the politeness he would show to a lady, with due regard for her feelings, and it makes him uncomfortable to be reminded that 'so slight a courtesy' is unusual.

The Plornish family represents the working class in *Little Dorrit*, paralleling the middle-class Meagles family and the upper-class Barnacles. Mrs Plornish is prematurely old, 'dragged at by poverty' and her many children, and Mr Plornish is covered in lime and is 'foolish in the face'. Although Dickens generally treats the Plornishes with sympathy, and his poor characters show a genuine concern for each other's welfare which his wealthy characters usually lack, he does not idealize the Plornishes in particular or the 'Bleeding Hearts' in general. Mr Plornish has a foolish and unexamined respect for Mr Dorrit's genteel pretence that his children do not work, and, as we shall see, the Bleeding Hearts have failings, chiefly deference to their 'betters', which contribute to their predicament.

The 'general misfortune' of the Yard is unemployment; Mr Plornish is one of many who are willing to work but can find none. The Barnacles, the rulers of the country, true to their 'great principle', do nothing about the problem. (Dickens is here attacking the belief, held by many though not all Victorian politicians, that governments not only could not but should not concern themselves with unemployment, and had no responsibility for ameliorating it.) Old inhabitants of the Yard are 'shut up' in the workhouse (the phrase suggests imprisonment), where they are 'much worse fed and lodged and treated altogether' than criminals. This was a common complaint in the 1850s, when improvements in prison conditions meant that convicted criminals had better treatment than people who had worked all their lives and were forced by poverty into the workhouse in old age. (We later find out that Plornish's father-in-law, Mr Nandy, is one of these.) Dickens uses Plornish's linguistic ineptitude – he says 'manufacturers' when he means 'malefactors' – to remind us of the glaring contrast between the wealth of the factory owners and the poverty of the workers. In Bleeding Heart Yard those who do find employment have to work 'day and night' just to 'keep body and soul together', and sometimes fail to earn enough to do even that.

This description of the plight of the poor is given in a long, confused monologue by Mr Plornish, who knows very well what poverty is, but cannot understand who is responsible for his predicament and what should be done about it. Dickens neatly renders Mr Plornish's bafflement through the image of a blind man trying to undo tangled thread, and indicates his own view of who is responsible for the poverty by ending chapter 12 with an allusion to the Circumlocution Office and beginning chapter 13 with a visit to the landlord of Bleeding Heart Yard, Mr Casby.

Mr Casby is one of the 'hunters of men' in *Little Dorrit*, a rapacious slum-landlord, 'formerly Town-agent to Lord Decimus Tite Barnacle', who charges extortionate rents to his tenants. He lives in a stifling house, which, like Mrs Clennam's, seems cut off from the outside world. Ironically, he has the reputation of a philanthropist, a benign 'patriarch'. (The word suggests the revered leader of a family or tribe in the Old Testament.) He has acquired this reputation because of an appearance which suggests 'rare wisdom and virtue' – an example, according to the narrator, of how 'in the great social Exhibition, accessories are often accepted in lieu of the internal character'. Casby is part of the great parade of social falsity in *Little Dorrit*, and one of the book's most successful confidence tricksters. He maintains his reputation for benignity by ensuring that his agent, Pancks, does the dirty work and gets the blame for the extortion. Pancks and Casby are one of the book's contrasting pairs: Casby serene, benevolent-looking, but in fact rapacious; and Pancks dirty, apparently an enthusiastic oppressor of his fellow man, but in fact, as we later discover, not what he seems. He is interestingly characterized in mechanical imagery, as though he were merely a machine in his master's control.

Dickens uses Pancks to raise explicitly, in a remarkable dialogue with Clennam (see ch. 13), an important question implicitly posed by *Little Dorrit*:

'But I like business,' said Pancks, getting on a little faster. 'What's a man made for?'

'For nothing else?' said Clennam.

Pancks put the counter question, 'What else?' It packed up, in the smallest compass, a weight that had rested on Clennam's life; and he made no answer.

'That's what I ask our weekly tenants,' said Pancks. 'Some of 'em will pull long faces to me, and say, Poor as you see us, master, we're always grinding, drudging, toiling, every minute we're awake. I say to them, What else are you made for? It shuts them up. They haven't a word to answer. What else are you made for? That clinches it.'

'Ah dear, dear, dear!' sighed Clennam.

'Here am I,' said Pancks, pursuing his argument with the weekly tenant. 'What else do you suppose I think I am made for? Nothing. Rattle me out of bed early, set me going, give me as short a time as you like to bolt my meals in, and keep me at it. Keep me always at it, and I'll keep you always at it, you keep somebody else always at it. There you are with the Whole Duty of Man in a commercial country.'

The Whole Duty of Man was a seventeenth-century handbook of religious devotion still widely circulated in Victorian England. The title derives from a passage in Ecclesiastes 12 which says that the whole duty of man is to 'fear God, and keep his commandments'. As Victorian readers were much more familiar with Christianity and the Bible than we are, Dickens was able to make these allusions knowing that their meaning and relevance would be perceived. In this case he uses the phrase to question and undermine Victorian civilization by reminding us how different life 'in a commercial country' is from life in a society which defines man's purpose and duties in Christian terms. In Bleeding Heart Yard, the only obligation people have to each other is to keep each other 'always at it'. Work has superseded religion and morality. What else is man made for? Clennam, whose life has been weighed down by 'grinding in a mill' can give no answer, and neither can the tenants in Bleeding Heart Yard whose life is one long drudgery. All are trapped in a commercial world which dominates their thoughts as well as their actions, so that the drudgery they endure makes them believe there is no alternative, however much they wish to find one. It is significant that Dickens chooses to raise the question in such a way as to concentrate our attention not simply on financial poverty (Clennam is well off), but also on a kind of mental imprisonment.

However, there are signs of liberation. Despite what he has just said, Pancks goes on to reveal that he has spare time and that he spends it collecting 'advertisements relative to next of kin', a hobby which we see is disinterested, because, although it involves 'an inclination to get money', it may benefit others and brings him no certain reward. We later find him acting on behalf of Little Dorrit simply because he finds 'something uncommon in the quiet little seamstress, which pleased him and provoked his curiosity' (ch. 35) – a motive free from self-interest. From the moment we first hear of this hobby, Pancks's claims to be a representative of economic man, acting solely to get money, begin to seem ironical. He is not at one with his role as Mr Casby's agent, and indeed seems to undermine it, until at last he removes all ambiguity, openly liberating himself, as we shall see. It is as though Dickens uses Pancks's split character to suggest his faith in human nature: whatever we say, we are simply unable to live only for work and money. And although Clennam can think of no immediate verbal answer to the question of what man is made for if not business, we know he is determined to escape from the world of his parents who 'weighed, measured and priced everything' (ch. 2), and he shows that determination by acts of generosity and kindness which defy the commercial ethic bluntly stated by Pancks: 'Take all you can get, and keep back all you can't be forced to give up' (ch. 23).

As though to emphasize this and to contrast it with the Circumlocutionary policy of doing nothing, one of Clennam's acts of generosity comes straight after his debate with Pancks in chapter 13: he accompanies Cavalletto, who has recently arrived in London (we last saw him halfway across France in chapter 11) to hospital after his accident, although he is a complete stranger. This incident calls to mind Christ's parable of the Good Samaritan, who also helps a stranger lying at the roadside. Christ tells the story in answer to the question, 'What shall I do to inherit eternal life?' The answer is to love God 'with all thy heart' and love 'thy neighbour as thyself'. The question, 'Who is my neighbour?' is answered by the parable, and Christ enjoins us to show mercy and compassion (Luke 10).

There was a vehement debate in Dickens's time about the relief of the poor. Some people, like Dickens, took the traditional religious view that we ought to love them as neighbours by treating them with mercy and compassion and doing whatever we could to help. Others, supported by influential economic theories, thought that acts of charity damaged the recipients by making them less self-reliant, less able to stand on their own feet. This view is contemptuously alluded to by Pancks and Clennam when they discuss Cavalletto's admission to hospital (ch. 23):

'It's pauperising a man, sir, I have been shown, to let him into a hospital?' said Pancks. And again blew off that remarkable sound.
'I have been shown so too,' said Clennam coldly.

To 'pauperise' a man is to make him a helpless and passive recipient of charity, unable to support himself. (Pancks and Clennam of course take for granted what is now often forgotten, that Victorian hospital treatment was usually free.) Dickens again alludes to the debate when, in connection with Mr Nandy's confinement in the workhouse, he compares the hard-hearted official provision for the poor with the generosity of the Good Samaritan (ch. 31).

When Cavalletto leaves hospital, Clennam helps him to find a room in Bleeding Heart Yard, and to find work with which to support himself. (There is another attack on orthodox economics in this example of private charity helping a man to help himself, rather than making him a pauper.) The presence of Cavalletto in Bleeding Heart Yard allows Dickens to create an important contrast between the Italian and his native English neighbours. Although poor, lame and afraid that Rigaud will catch up with him, Cavalletto is cheerful, 'easy and hopeful'. He supports himself with odd jobs and by happily carving wooden flowers to sell. When not at work he plays with the children, sits in the sun and laughs – extraordinary behaviour in Bleeding Heart Yard, and it attracts and refreshes Pancks by 'force of contrast' (ch. 25). The contrast is the good news brought by John Baptist, the revelation that man is truly not made solely to be 'kept at it', and can enjoy and find significance in something other than work – indeed, even work can be enjoyable.

Cavalletto lives happily in the poverty and misery of Bleeding Heart Yard, just as he lived free in spirit in the Marseilles prison. He is free from the imprisoned grimness of Victorian England, and can suffer poverty without letting it mark his soul. But the contrast also deepens the gloomy impression given by the depiction of England in *Little Dorrit*. Is Dickens suggesting that only a foreigner can escape English gloom, or does he imply that English imprisonments are self-inflicted, not inevitable, and can be escaped by a change of heart? However we answer these questions there is no doubt that the appearance of a 'true son of Italy' (ch. 1) in Bleeding Heart Yard brings a valuable alternative possibility into the world of the novel. Not, of course, that the Bleeding Hearts see things in that way – they share the insularity of Mr Meagles, and are content to patronize Cavalletto and treat him like a baby. They are confident of their superiority to foreigners because they have been persuaded by the Barnacles that 'it was a sort of Divine visitation upon a foreigner that he was not an Englishman, and that all kinds of calamities happened to his country because it did things that England did not, and did not do things that England did' (ch. 23). So they despise foreigners as poor, oppressed and lacking in independence of spirit – as they themselves actually are. This deluded habit of seeing in others what you cannot allow yourself to recognize in your own life helps to preserve the confined world of Bleeding Heart Yard, which, as the presence of Cavalletto suggests, is as much a matter of mental as physical poverty.

Dickens's treatment of Bleeding Heart Yard is a remarkable attack on the English capacity for living with the intolerable by self-deception. It probably now needs some effort of the historical imagination to recall the overweening sense of national superiority which pervaded mid-Victorian England at the height of her economic power, but it is easy to see that Dickens did not share it, any more than he shared the equally characteristic Victorian belief that working and getting money summed up the whole life and duty of man. He treats such beliefs in *Little Dorrit* as signs and causes of social and individual imprisonment, and represents the country which lives by them as a Bleeding Heart Yard.

Doyce and Gowan (chs. 16, 17 and others)

Beginning in chapter 16, Dickens introduces an important theme, the place of the creative imagination in the imprisoned world of *Little Dorrit*, by contrasting two characters, Daniel Doyce, the engineer, and Henry Gowan, the painter. We first met Doyce in chapter 10 being ejected (ironically) from the Circumlocution Office by Mr Meagles, as though he were a 'public offender', after the failure of their attempt, over twelve years, to persuade the Barnacles of the value of Doyce's invention. In chapter 16 Doyce's career up to his rejection by the Circumlocution Office is briefly summarized in a chance conversation between Doyce and Clennam which ultimately leads to their entering into partnership. (This is one of the voluntary associations in the book which indicates affinities between characters.)

Doyce is a man of humble origins, the son of a north-country blacksmith, who has risen by native genius and hard work to his present position as an engineer. To achieve this he has studied and practised both at home and abroad, where he is, of course, much better treated than in England. The narrator describes Doyce as a plain man of 'great modesty and good sense', accustomed 'to combine what was original and daring in conception with what was patient and minute in execution'. His devotion to useful work is the opposite of the Circumlocution Office's 'How not to do it', and an expression of his conviction that life is necessarily strenuous: 'You hold your life on the condition that to the last you shall struggle hard for it.' Although thwarted by the Circumlocution Office, Doyce is not discouraged because he knows his invention is valuable, whatever the Barnacles do – 'The thing is as true as it ever was.' This 'calm knowledge' gives Doyce a strength of character which derives from his lack of concern for himself, his capacity for disinterested activity. He is one of the characters in *Little Dorrit* who are not obsessed by themselves, and who can act for the benefit of others.

Daniel Doyce is directly contrasted with a very different figure, Henry Gowan the painter, a complex character who plays an important part in the novel. We first meet Gowan in chapter 17, seeing him through the eyes of Arthur Clennam, whose immediate impressions are that he is a well-dressed 'sprightly' gentleman who unintentionally betrays something of himself by the way he casually kicks stones into the water while waiting for the Twickenham ferry: 'There was something in his way of spurning them out of their places with his heel, and getting them into the required position, that Clennam thought had an air of cruelty in it.' This is an interesting example of Dickens's use of gesture to reveal the inner life of a character whose consciousness is not directly rendered. It also anticipates and sums up Gowan's way of dealing with Clennam as a rival in love, as we shall see, and lays the foundation of a character who, under cover of a disarming frankness and false intimacy, often causes and takes pleasure in others' discomfort and pain, usually in subtle and apparently polite ways which make it very difficult for his victims to be sure of what is happening and to respond (see, for example, the conversation at Hampton Court in chapter 26).

Along with this trait of refined cruelty goes a habit of talking about others in an apparently engaging way which blurs true moral perceptions: '. . . everybody whom this Gowan knew was either more or less of an ass, or more or less of a knave; but was, notwithstanding, the most loveable, the most engaging, the simplest, truest, kindest, dearest, best fellow that ever lived' (ch. 17). Gowan implies that he carefully conducts a kind of moral book-keeping, adding up with precision everyone's good and evil actions. (This is an interesting intrusion of commercial practice into the moral life, which recalls Mrs Clennam's habit of keeping accounts with God.) The result, he affirms, is 'that there is much less difference than you are inclined to suppose between an honest man and a scoundrel'. The effect of this is that while Gowan 'seemed to be scrupulously finding good in most men, he did in reality lower it where it was, and set it up where it was not' (ch. 17).

Gowan's attitude to his profession contrasts sharply with Doyce's – he has 'a slight, careless amateur way with him' (ch. 17). Doyce comments that Gowan is only 'a sort of an artist' because 'he has sauntered into the Arts at a leisurely Pall-Mall pace . . . and I doubt if they care to be taken quite so coolly'. (Pall-Mall is a street at the centre of the fashionable district in London where the gentlemen's clubs are to be found, and Doyce is hinting at the social origins in gentlemanly idleness of Gowan's casual approach to his art.) But Gowan takes matters further by asserting in one of a series of arguments with Clennam that no one really takes art seriously. Artists, in his view, are merely impostors who create in order to sell their work for as much as possible. Their profession is a 'trade', with nothing difficult about it. Their claims that they genuinely devote themselves to their art and that it is strenuously demanding are merely 'hocus-pocus', a juggler's pretence (ch. 34). (The implication, of course, is that he is less of a humbug than the rest because he admits this.) In Gowan's opinion, this also applies to social life generally, because not only painters but 'writers, patriots, all the rest who have stands in the market' are confidence tricksters, and the more successful they are the greater the deceit. And so Gowan dismisses Doyce, who has not become rich and is therefore not successful, as a kind of naive innocent, 'so fresh, so green' (ch. 26).

Gowan's view of society as one great confidence trick recalls Rigaud's belief that lawyers, politicians and financiers live by their wits, as he does, and the deceit is, as Clennam points out, most practised by the 'political gentlemen who condescend to keep the Circumlocution Office' (ch. 26). Gowan is, of course, related to the Barnacles by family connections as well as moral affinity. In a passage characteristic of Dickens's satiric wit, the narrator tells us that Gowan's father, originally a diplomat, had been 'pensioned off as a Commissioner of nothing particular somewhere or other, and had died at this post with his drawn salary in his hand, nobly defending it to the last extremity' (ch. 17). His widow received a large pension and a free apartment at Hampton Court.

Henry Gowan has a small unearned income, but is not otherwise provided for by his relatives, and so takes up painting, 'partly because he had always had an idle knack that way, and partly to grieve the souls of the Barnacles-in-Chief who had not provided for him' (ch. 17). Why should that grieve the Barnacles? Because, as gentlemen, they are precluded from earning their living by practising one of 'the lower Arts', as Mrs Gowan calls painting, and should never be more than amateurs if they do dally with an art (ch. 26). However, despite using his profession to needle the Barnacles, Gowan is a defender of the Circumlocution Office because it's 'a school for gentlemen', although he knows that it 'may ultimately shipwreck everybody and everything' (ch. 26). Unlike Doyce, he is of course favoured by the Circumlocution Office – he receives the patronage and approval of the Barnacles for paintings which the public does not value, apparently as a reward for not taking his art seriously and being a gentleman first and last.

Gowan and Doyce are opposites. Doyce is a hard-working, creative, dedicated man, devoted to the truth, not an egotist, and capable of disinterested and useful action. Gowan is an idle dilettante, full of cynicism and pretences, obsessed with himself, incapable of creating anything valuable, but with a deep animus against the arts generally. The Circumlocution Office thwarts Doyce because he is useful, and favours Gowan because he empties art of anything but genteel pretences. Gowan's version of art reflects the circumlocutionary world to which he belongs, and offers no escape from it.

Love (chs. 13, 16 and others)

There is not much love in *Little Dorrit*, but what there is is important because it might offer an escape from the generally oppressive and miserable world of the novel. However, love in Book One of *Little Dorrit* is always frustrated and disappointed, and the dominant tone is of pain, sadness and loss. The main concentration is on Arthur Clennam and Amy Dorrit's parallel and contrasting misadventures in love, usually treated with great psychological subtlety. We first see Clennam in chapter 2 as 'a grave, dark man of forty' abstractedly looking at Pet Meagles, a 'lovely girl' of twenty, as she walks away from him. This incident, as we later find out, anticipates their whole relationship – he makes no serious effort to win Pet, and loses her. For Clennam love is, of course, a possible way out of the miserable loveless world he has inherited from his parents, and, as we saw at the end of chapter 3, he is still able to remember and re-live his hopeless love for his childhood sweetheart and to begin to 'dream', stimulated by the news that she is now a widow and available to him. (The whole passage repays close reading. Dickens artfully brings together the three women who are important in Clennam's love-life: his childhood sweetheart; Pet Meagles, who reminded him of his childhood sweetheart; and Little Dorrit, who is promptly ruled out as a lover by Mrs Flintwinch.) The question is whether Clennam will be able to do any more than dream, or whether his upbringing has deprived him of will and purpose, as he thinks.

Clennam's first disappointment comes in chapter 13, when he re-visits the home of his childhood sweetheart, Flora, daughter of Mr Casby the patriarch and widow of Mr Finching. (This episode is founded on an incident in Dickens's life; for details see '*Little Dorrit* and Dickens's Life', Part Three, pp. 120–21). Flora is one of the greatest achievements of characterization in *Little Dorrit*. Her language has an extraordinary poetic vitality. Like some other things in this novel, it is at first bewildering. But it soon becomes apparent that despite her disregard for logic, Flora's stream of consciousness makes sense, even if it is not conventionally expressed. She also enjoys her flights of fancy, and is one of the few good-natured characters in the novel, as we later come to see. To Clennam, however, who expects to find the romantic and enchanting figure of his youthful dreams, Flora is a dreadful disappointment, as she herself is acute enough to realize and frank enough to point out, to Clennam's embarrassment. The effect is partly comic, as Flora goes on incongruously and delightedly pretending that they are still young lovers, fat and forty though she may be, and she renews this flirtatiousness to great comic effect whenever she sees Clennam again. But it is also sad, as we can see that Flora really does wish to renew the relationship and that Clennam has had his one hope destroyed.

A grimly comic note is added by the appearance of Mr Finching's Aunt, a demented old woman with no name of her own who shows violent hatred for Arthur and disconcerts him with random statements which make no sense in this context, although conveying her malignity clearly enough. 'Mr F.'s Aunt,' who lives in a world of her own and exudes hatred, is a horribly comic version of Mrs Clennam. (There seems to be no escape for Arthur.) Her regular appearances paired with Flora ensure that Flora's persistent and embarrassing devotion to Arthur is accompanied by Mr F.'s Aunt's unappeasable hostility to him, a contradictory and confusing combination. Its immediate effect on Clennam is to send him back to his lodgings to think again about the emptiness of his life, 'with all its misdirection and little happiness'. (The narrator links this review of his life with the previous ones by recalling the 'blackened forest of chimneys' Clennam had seen from the window of his old room, in chapter 3.) Brutally stripped of his romantic hopes, Clennam sees his life as a dying fire, or, in a striking image, as 'like descending a green tree in fruit and flower, and seeing all the branches wither and drop off one by one, as he came down towards them'. At this moment of justified despair in chapter 13 comes an answer (which he does not understand) to a rhetorical question (which he thinks has no answer):

'From the unhappy suppression of my youngest days, through the rigid and unloving home that followed them, through my departure, my long exile, my return, my mother's welcome, my intercourse with her since, down to the afternoon of this day with poor Flora ... what have I found!'

His door was softly opened, and these spoken words startled him, and came as if they were an answer:

'Little Dorrit.'

Clennam does not see this incident as we may do. Although he thinks of Little Dorrit a great deal, he views her not as a lover but as a child, a little mother who looks after her family and is grateful for the help he gives her. The ties between them, he thinks, are those of 'innocent reliance on one hand, and affectionate protection on the other; ties of compassion, respect, unselfish interest, gratitude and pity' (ch. 16). Dickens makes it easy for us to see how this arises naturally from Clennam's initial interest in Amy as a 'subdued child' in Mrs Clennam's household, such as he had been himself, and from his wish to do good to someone who clearly deserves help and respect for her extraordinary care for her family. So he thinks of her at most as a kind of adopted daughter. For a lover he turns his thoughts to another, more attractive young woman, the beautiful, childish Pet Meagles, who had reminded him of his childhood sweetheart. (This partial clinging to the past is another example of the care Dickens takes to make Clennam's motivation convincing.) Characteristically, however, his self-doubt persuades him that because of his age and deficiencies of character, as he sees them, he should not fall in love and try to win her. This decision leads at once to a mood of conflict and depression, even a wish to die, 'to flow away monotonously like the river, and to compound for its insensibility to happiness with its insensibility to pain' (ch. 16). As Dickens takes care to place this decision before Clennam's discovery that Pet already has a suitor, we can see that he gives up not because the opposition is too strong for him, but because renunciation and defeat are part of his nature.

Further suffering follows as he stands by and watches his rival in love, Henry Gowan, woo and win Pet, despite her misgivings and the opposition of her parents. Daniel Doyce, as so often a reliable observer, compares the wooing to the trapping of a helpless animal; in chapter 26 he talks of Gowan 'with a net about the pretty and affectionate creature whom he will never make happy'. Clennam does nothing to try to avert this disaster; he merely attempts to persuade himself (unsuccessfully) that, against all the evidence, he is not in love with Pet, that Gowan is not as bad as he seems and is not deliberately tormenting him, and that the prospective marriage is more promising than it looks. As Dickens tells the story through Clennam's consciousness, this experience of self-inflicted pain and loss, mixed with futile self-deception and unavailing attempts to find peace in the natural world (see, for example, the beginning of chapter 28) adds to our sense that Clennam is still emotionally imprisoned. We may think Pet unsuitable for Clennam, but that is no consolation to him, and he is left with nothing but a 'miserable blank' in his heart (ch. 34).

A similar tone of sadness and loss mixed with comedy which does not relieve but rather intensifies the sadness is found in the contrasting but intertwined love-plot centred on Little Dorrit. Dickens tells this story in a different way. We are given no privileged insight into Little Dorrit's consciousness (unlike Clennam's), and have to be alert for the often subtly expressed signs of her feelings.

Amy's admirer since childhood has been John Chivery, who parallels Flora's place in Arthur Clennam's life, except that his feelings for Amy are never reciprocated. Chivery's fortunes, or rather misfortunes, as a lover are concentrated in chapter 18, where he is rejected by Little Dorrit before he can get as far as an explicit declaration of love, in an encounter which is distressing to both in different ways. Chivery, the 'sentimental son of a turnkey', is partly a ludicrous figure, with his absurd clothes and over-dressed romantic language, but his pretensions do not conceal his genuine feelings for Amy, and so he is a sad figure as well as a funny one – he is treated with too much sympathy simply to be laughed at, and of course Amy does not laugh at him at all. Indeed, when she is surprised by him on the Iron Bridge after avoiding him for a long time, she starts away with 'an expression in her face of fright and something like dislike that caused him unutterable dismay'. This is one of the moments which help to prevent Amy from seeming too good to be true; we can see that she is capable of hostile feelings and can lose her self-control. She only recovers when prompted by Chivery's 'delicacy' in asking whether he may 'say something' to her – obviously it will be a declaration of love – which allows her the opportunity to reject him unambiguously and finally while sparing his feelings as far as possible.

The chapter ends with the disconsolate Chivery imagining his early death and drafting the inscription for his tombstone, a comic parallel to Clennam's wish to die at the end of chapter 16. However, we later see him still alive and devoted to Amy in chapter 25, helping Pancks to search for the Dorrit fortune. Chivery's absurdities ensure that we do not see him as a serious lover for Little Dorrit, but the genuineness of his feelings does show that she can inspire love, even though Arthur Clennam does not reciprocate her love for him.

Little Dorrit's love for Clennam is delicately treated as a rule. Since Clennam firmly persists in thinking of Little Dorrit as a child, not a lover, her feelings have to be expressed indirectly and covertly. It is clear that her respect and gratitude to Clennam for his kindness to her and her family are the foundation of her love for him. Dickens makes it easy for us to see that the harshness of her life and the weight of the burdens she has to carry account for the extremity of her gratitude (in order to express it, in chapter 14, she risks having to stay out on the streets of London all night). The development of this gratitude into love is not traced in detail, but there is an interesting exchange in chapter 14 which suggests that she is already unhappy in the child-role that Clennam wants to keep her in. By now Clennam, who in chapter 9 was able to restrain himself from calling Amy a child, addresses her as 'my poor child' or 'my child' without thinking. However, he does notice that a 'slight shade of distress fell upon her, at his so often calling her a child', and agrees not to do it again, explaining that he 'wanted a tender word, and could think of no other'. Later on in the same chapter Little Dorrit has a nocturnal encounter with a prostitute who thinks her a child because of her diminutive size and addresses her as one, and Amy makes no protest at all, indeed tries to speak as though she really were a child. This contrasting response suggests that her distress comes from being treated as a child by Clennam, and not simply from being treated as a child.

Clennam of course goes on thinking of Little Dorrit as a child even if he no longer addresses her as one, and is disconcerted when he hears from Mrs Chivery that the young woman he thinks of as 'a kind of domesticated fairy' is loved by John Chivery (ch. 22). This leads to another encounter on the Iron Bridge (paralleling and contrasting with the Chivery episode in the previous chapter), during which we see, although Clennam doesn't, that Amy is in love with him. A discussion of the consolation she brings her father in prison leads to her asking Clennam, 'If you were in prison, could I bring such comfort to you?' His reply, 'Yes, Little Dorrit, I am sure of it!' causes 'a tremor on her lip, and a passing shadow of great agitation on her face', which Clennam characteristically thinks is because 'her mind was with her father'. Ironically, her distress simply reinforces his view of her as 'a poor child', and although he thinks of her more and more, it is always in the same way. We are later to see a further irony in this: it is not until Little Dorrit does visit Clennam in prison that he is able to see that she loves him.

Amy's predicament is worsened in two subsequent encounters, in both of which she is unable to express her feelings directly. The first, with Flora, causes her distress because she is understandably misled by Flora's wild talk of her romantic passion for Clennam into believing that Clennam loves Flora (ch. 23). Flora notices Little Dorrit's pallor and faintness, but naturally doesn't understand her reactions as we do. Amy's belief that she has a successful rival in love parallels Clennam's experience with Pet. Amy's response, though sad, is less depressed and more creative than Clennam's. She tells Maggy 'The Story of the Princess' (ch. 24), the tale of a tiny woman who treasures until her death the shadow of someone who has gone 'quite out of reach'. This story within a story is a subtle way of indirectly expressing Little Dorrit's feelings, and it contributes to our sense that she is emotionally stronger than Clennam. Unlike him, she does not attempt to reduce her pain by self-deception, and she transforms her feelings into a work of art, which gives them full, if disguised, expression.

The second encounter is with Clennam himself (ch. 32) and is perhaps more painful, partly because she is forced into contact with the man she has been avoiding, and partly because Clennam unintentionally says the worst possible things. Blinded by 'the light of her domestic story', Clennam reverts to calling her 'my child' again, and also says, 'My own Little Dorrit,' words that might mean love, but are an expression of mere compassion. He goes on to confide in Amy that he is not in love with Flora or Pet, and has renounced love because of his age – 'Always think of me as quite an old man.'

Dickens evidently decided to make sure that no reader missed the point of this scene. The narrator makes comments which represent Dickens at his least subtle. For example: 'O! if he had known, if he had known! If he could have seen the dagger in his hand, and the cruel wounds it struck in the faithful bleeding breast of his Little Dorrit!' Such comments, and the violence of the imagery used, reveal an authentically Victorian pleasure in extreme pathos and the blatant effect. They are likely to have the opposite effect on the modern reader from that intended: we may well be suspicious of the excitement derived from imagining pain; we may even laugh. Dickens is capable both of extreme subtlety and extreme blatancy, which cannot be reconciled, though they may be explained as an attempt to write at several levels of sophistication so as to reach the widest possible audience. Nevertheless, this novel, like all novels, can survive occasional lapses like these which do not substantially detract from the generally subtle and painful story of Little Dorrit's disappointed love.

Father and Daughter (ch. 19)

Little Dorrit's rejection of John Chivery's advances has an immediate consequence in the short but intense chapter 19, most of which is devoted to a crisis in the relation between the Father of the Marshalsea and his daughter. How important this relation is we can see from Dickens's decision to develop it before he has introduced us to all the main settings and characters in the novel. The chapter begins with Mr Dorrit contentedly playing his 'courtly' and 'condescending' role as Father of the Marshalsea, patronizing his broken brother Frederick and receiving 'presentations'. His equanimity is suddenly disturbed by a few gruff words from Mr Chivery, who apparently resents his son's lack of success as a suitor. This impels Mr Dorrit to remind Amy that he is 'unfortunately dependent' on men like Mr Chivery 'every hour in the day', and to hint that she should lead John Chivery on, so as to ensure her father's comfort in the jail. Mr Dorrit's shame at the disguised suggestion he cannot allow himself to make openly is subtly revealed by his physical and verbal mannerisms, such as the Freudian slip of 'father' for 'brother' in the story he tells, and by his tailing off into silence without completing a sentence.

Little Dorrit's refusal is entirely unspoken, and conveyed without even a gesture: 'His voice died away, as if she could not bear the pain of hearing him, and her hand had gradually crept to his lips.' Her pain is not described, but only hinted at with the conditional 'as if'. Even the slow gesture of putting her hand to her father's lips is only imagined by the narrator as a possibility, not described as an action which took place (she remains motionless with her arm round his neck). Dickens could easily have made the gesture happen, but instead chooses to make us feel how much meaning can be conveyed by silence and stillness, guiding our response with the narrator's imagination. The absence of sound and movement helps to fix the subsequent tableau: 'For a little while, there was a dead silence and stillness; and he remained shrunk in his chair, and she remained with her arm round his neck, and her head bowed down upon his shoulder.'

This painful silence is one of the most eloquent moments in the novel, a remarkable example of how Dickens can make us feel and understand what is happening between characters into whose thoughts we have no direct access, and who do not even speak or move. Little Dorrit must not give way to her father's wishes if she is to maintain her integrity, especially as a lover. And yet a spoken refusal would require open and precise mention of a request so humiliating and shameful that her father cannot bring himself to do more than hint at it. Amy's solution, silence accompanied by a loving gesture, allows her to keep her integrity and to maintain the strength of character we have seen in her habitual self-reliance and her moral and financial support of her family. It is also consistent with her characteristic reticence and forbearance, and her love and pity for her father. It allows him to preserve some self-respect while he continues to play the only role he can, that of Father of the Marshalsea, which he promptly resumes with all its self-deceptions, self-ishnesses and assertions of his superiority to others. However, we have been shown that despite 'jail-rot' he can feel shame at his behaviour and recognize that he is 'a poor prisoner'. However unreflective he is, he has some real sense of what he has become. However much he goes on imposing on himself and others we see that there is some depth of character beneath the role-playing, and we may even find him something of a tragic figure with whose sufferings we can sympathize.

The cruelty of her father's imprisonment is powerfully rendered through Little Dorrit's consciousness at the end of the chapter. She contrasts the freedom of the natural world with the 'gloomy and contracted' Marshalsea, which she sees as 'a living grave . . . with her father in it', a horrible image which makes us think of him as buried alive. It is characteristic of Amy that she reconciles herself to her father's defects by believing that she has never really known him because she has never seen him as he was before his imprisonment – 'No, no, I have never seen him in my life!' If we recall what Mr Dorrit was like when we first saw him on his entry to the Marshalsea we may well not share this view, but we may see it as an understandable reaction to Amy's discovery of the full extent of her father's present degradation; she has to believe that he was a different man once.

The effect of this remarkable chapter is to leave us with a heightened sense of the characters of Amy and her father, and of the relation between them. We are made to feel how deeply affected Mr Dorrit is by 'jail-rot', with his self-deceptions, selfishness and ruthless exploitation of his daughter. And yet we also see that he has vestiges of conscience and self-knowledge, and that he suffers intensely in confinement, despite his success in the role of Father of the Marshalsea. This helps us to think of Amy's heroic love and pity for her father as something more than emotions wasted on a wholly undeserving man. We also see that she has no illusions about what her father has become, and that helps us to think of her as a character with a sense of reality and a capacity for moral judgement. And, most important of all, we see that she can quietly but successfully resist exploitation by her father, and defend her integrity.

Marriage and Society (chs. 20, 33 and others)

There is one wedding and one prevented marriage in Book One of *Little Dorrit*. The wedding is between Pet Meagles and Henry Gowan, and the averted marriage might have taken place between Fanny Dorrit and Edmund Sparkler. Both relationships take us into 'Society', the social life of the rich, aristocratic and powerful. We have already seen the life of the poor in Bleeding Heart Yard, and of the middle classes in the Clennam and Meagles households, and of course we have encountered the Barnacles in their political and administrative roles at the Circumlocution Office. The Society chapters complete Dickens's panorama of the social classes in *Little Dorrit*. For convenience I shall refer briefly to some of the Gowan chapters (17, 26 and 34), and shall then consider at greater length the treatment of marriage in chapter 20, in which Amy Dorrit pays her unexpected visit to Mrs Merdle, and in chapter 33, which brings together Mrs Merdle and Mrs Gowan. Although they have sombre undertones, these chapters are bracingly satirical.

We first meet a member of Society socially at Mr Meagles's in chapter 17, when Henry Gowan brings the 'well connected' if totally stupid Clarence Barnacle to dinner. Despite his experiences in the Circumlocution Office, Mr Meagles loves a lord, and welcomes his fatuous guest with 'peculiar complacency'. (Dickens satirizes this weakness by giving the aristocrats whose names Mr Meagles reverently recites absurd surnames like 'Toozellem'. He also implicates the reader by making the narrator remind us that false deference to rank is 'a weakness which none of us need go into the next street to find'.) Despite Mr Meagles's expectations however, the dinner party is not a success – the presence of Clarence Barnacle makes 'the eating of the dinner, like the dinner itself ... lukewarm, insipid, overdone', and Mr Meagles is ill at ease and not himself.

The Gowan connection is continued in chapter 26 when Gowan takes Clennam on an uncomfortable visit to his mother at Hampton Court Palace, a depressing 'red brick dungeon' (we notice that this is another kind of prison), full of dissatisfaction, arrogance, political opinions about five hundred years behind the times, and the frigid falsity characteristic of Society in *Little Dorrit*. The marriage of Pet and Gowan at last happens in chapter 34, at a ceremony attended by numerous patronizing Barnacle relatives of the Gowans who make Mr Meagles feel 'low and unhappy', although he manages to persuade himself afterwards that the 'high company' has done him good. One thread that links these episodes is the unhappiness which moving in Society brings to Meagles and Clennam.

Amy Dorrit makes her entry to Society in chapter 20. One of her duties as 'Little Mother' to her family is to look after the welfare of her sister Fanny, who works as a dancer at a not very distinguished theatre. (Her nominal chaperon, her uncle Frederick, is of course oblivious to what is going on around him, and quite useless as a protector.) We need to know that it was common for actresses in Victorian theatres to be kept as mistresses by wealthy gentlemen. By conventional moral standards, such women become 'fallen women', not received in respectable society. That is the unspoken peril which surrounds Fanny, and which Dickens can leave unspoken because it was so well known in both Victorian life and literature. On hearing in chapter 20 that Fanny has been given a bracelet (she says it was given by a lady), the Victorian reader would assume that she is receiving presents from admirers and is in danger of becoming a kept woman, thus losing her reputation and marriage prospects. Some such fears impel Little Dorrit to make her first visit to the theatre, though characteristically she does not allow herself to express them directly; all she says is that she has not been 'quite easy' on Fanny's account since hearing about the bracelet.

It turns out that these unspoken fears are well-founded – Fanny has an admirer who has been making advances. But she has done the proper thing, protected her virtue and held out for marriage. From a conventional Victorian point of view, that would be the end of the problem. Dickens raises the conventional anxiety and promptly resolves it in order to concentrate our attention on Fanny's real predicament. She is, we discover, in genuine moral danger, but not of the conventional kind. Her wealthy and distinguished admirer (who we later find out is an almost complete idiot, as she well knows) had been on the point of proposing marriage when his mother, Mrs Merdle, intervened to prevent it. (It was acceptable for a young wealthy man to keep an actress as a mistress, but intolerable for him to marry someone beneath his social position and without money.) Mrs Merdle, we discover, has bought Fanny off by a combination of presents (money, dresses and the bracelet) and the threat (sweetly and politely made) that her son would be disinherited if he married Fanny. As Fanny accepts this, we can see that she has no feelings for her admirer, but is only interested in his money and the social status that goes with it. Little Dorrit is brought in to observe that Fanny is characteristically engaged in a battle to maintain her family pride, which has been wounded by Mrs Merdle's refusal to countenance her as a daughter-in-law, and is trying to hit back by taking 'presents' from her and defying her at the interview she has insisted on.

This is the shadow of the Marshalsea wall on Fanny. Despite all her advantages of good looks and vitality, she is locked into a trap like her father's: all that matters is money and social status; marriage is a means of achieving both, and she will accept the advances of a wealthy idiot to get them. Frustrated, she asserts the family pride against those who look down on her social position and poverty, and, like her father, accepts 'presents'. Her inner misery under the social pretences is revealed at the end of the chapter when she quarrels with Amy. However, her distress, unlike Amy's or Clennam's, is certainly not caused by hopeless love, but by a thwarted passion for social status which has the intensity of love, and replaces it in her life.

The other main figure in chapter 20 is Mrs Merdle, the representative of Society and wife of the wealthy and influential Mr Merdle. By introducing us to the Merdle household through Mrs Merdle's treatment of Fanny and marriage, Dickens makes Society's lack of true feeling its most immediate characteristic. The first thing we see in Mrs Merdle's grand house, after the powdered footmen, is a parrot 'on the outside of a golden cage'. Dickens uses this bird to remarkable effect, to represent and to satirize the behaviour of people in Society. The bird puts itself into 'many strange upside-down postures' which imitate the pretences and moral contortions of Society figures, 'climbing upon golden wires'. Whenever Mrs Merdle says something particularly pretentious, the parrot laughs. The movements of its 'cruel beak and black tongue' add a note of grotesque menace which seems to underlie the polite surface of Society.

Mrs Merdle herself is a compound of pretences and pretensions. Her 'young and fresh' appearance is not natural but manufactured. Repression and confinement are suggested by the 'rich white fillet' she wears over her head and under her chin, which is 'curbed up so tight and close by that laced bridle'. She makes the most of her left hand, which is whiter and plumper than the other, and uses her eye-glass as a means of putting down Amy and Fanny. She talks 'as coldly as a woman of snow', as though 'apparently addressing some abstraction of Society'. Along with this goes an affectation of a liking for the simple life as lived by 'the Savages in the Tropic seas' and a pretence of weakness and susceptibility to emotion which do not conceal her complete lack of feeling and her polite but ruthless efficiency in sparring with and disposing of Fanny, in the interests of her family's social position.

Mrs Merdle discusses marriage again in chapter 33, in a contrasting but related interview with Mrs Gowan, who has come to see her because she represents and expresses Society so well. We know that Pet Meagles's prospective marriage to Henry Gowan is opposed by her parents because of well-founded doubts about Gowan's character. Mrs Gowan by contrast, approves the match because of its financial advantages – Mr Meagles will pay Gowan's debts 'down upon the altar-railing', a phrase which sharpens our sense of the mercenariness of the motive by making us think of the money being paid at the wedding ceremony in church. (We also notice the difference between the treatment of Gowan's debts and Mr Dorrit's.) In addition, Gowan will have a good income and financial expectations from Mr Meagles which will relieve his mother of contributing to his support. However, despite these advantages, the wedding is to a social inferior, so Mrs Gowan feels obliged to protect her family's position by pretending that she regrets the marriage, and that she only agreed to it, Pet having fascinated her son, after much opposition and with a sense of sacrifice. Mrs Gowan imposes this fiction on Mrs Clennam in chapter 26 with characteristic insolence, getting the Meagleses' name wrong and asserting that 'such people will do anything for the honour of an alliance', and she repeats this to Mrs Merdle in chapter 33 with gratifying results.

Mrs Merdle, as 'Priestess of Society', rules that Society requires that a man should gain by marriage and, having ascertained precisely how much Henry Gowan is to gain, thinks that 'this was a sufficiently good catch'. She nevertheless says what is expected of her, that she sympathizes with Mrs Gowan's misfortune in having a son 'marrying among people not in Society'. Both Mrs Gowan and Mrs Merdle know perfectly well that this is a mere pretence, and know that Society will see through it too. But keeping up forms and pretences is an essential part of Society behaviour, cloaking the avarice and lack of feeling which are its prime characteristics. In marriage, love is of no consequence. What matters is money. Pet Meagles, though socially inferior and of course to be patronized as such, is an acceptable marriage partner because she is wealthy. Fanny Dorrit, at this stage in the novel, has no money to make up for her inferior social position, and is therefore not acceptable. At the apex of the social pyramid in *Little Dorrit* we find a 'matrimonial market' in which marriage is treated as a cynical and loveless matter of mercenary convenience. We are to see the consequences in Book Two.

Mr Merdle (chs. 21 and 33)

Mr Merdle is an immensely rich man at the centre of the commercial and financial system and therefore of Society. No one knows precisely what his business is, except that he is 'in everything' and makes a great deal of money. To his house come the most powerful men in England, from the royal Court, the City of London, Parliament, the Law, the Church, the Civil Service, the Army and the Navy. Dickens does not give these men individual names but calls them 'Bar', 'Treasury', 'Bishop', and so on, as though to make certain that we see them not as individuals but as representatives of a system. One after the other these magnates court Mr Merdle, flatter him, and seek financial favours in language appropriate to their positions.

Dickens treats this deference to wealth satirically and undermines it by various means. For instance, there are the disrespectful comments of the narrator, who describes these powerful men as 'all the magnates that keep us going, and sometimes trip us up', and deflates the dignity of the occasion by referring, for example, to the absurd appearance of a countess 'who was secluded somewhere in the core of an immense dress, to which she was in the proportion of the heart to the overgrown cabbage'. More important is the undermining of Bishop, who betrays that he is just as worldly as the others, while trying to pretend otherwise and appear rather poor. The jaunty posture he adopts while talking to Mr Merdle suggests that he thinks of his apron, part of the distinctive dress of a bishop, as 'a mere form'. We might expect Christians to be sceptical of money-worship in view of Christ's teaching (which the narrator recalls) that it is easier for a camel to pass through the eye of a needle than for a rich man to enter the Kingdom of Heaven (Matthew 19), but in *Little Dorrit* the representative of organized religion cultivates Mr Merdle as assiduously as the rest. Dickens introduces these references to religion partly to satirize the Church for ignoring the precepts of its founder, and partly to undermine Society by emphasizing how unchristian the worship of money is. (This is another occasion on which Dickens contrasts Victorian practice with New Testament principle.) The only magnate who is not venal is Physician, who shows no deference to Mr Merdle.

The most prominent feature of the magnificence of the Merdle household is Mrs Merdle. Dickens audaciously represents her by her splendid but unfeeling bosom, which he repeatedly describes as a jewel-stand displaying Mr Merdle's wealth and attracting 'general admiration'. Not surprisingly, given Victorian literary conventions, contemporary critics of *Little Dorrit* objected strongly to this frank mention of a bosom in a novel. (The fashion of the period for married women was very *décolleté*, but it was considered bad taste to refer to such things in a work of literature.) Dickens deliberately breaks this convention to make his satirical point. Instead of being something to provide nourishment for a baby (Mrs Merdle's idiotic son is mentioned next to the coldness of the bosom, as though to suggest why something has gone wrong there), something 'to repose upon', or something sexually attractive, Mrs Merdle's bosom becomes, to universal applause, something cold and hard which Mr Merdle has bought to display his wealth. What better symbol of the perversion of human feeling into an obsession with money could there be?

The most surprising feature of the Merdle establishment is the 'great and fortunate' Mr Merdle himself, who, though devoted to Society, 'hardly seemed to enjoy himself much, and was mostly to be found against walls and behind doors', looking reserved and uneasy and 'clasping his wrists as if he were taking himself into custody'. Why should Mr Merdle appear to arrest himself? What is the mysterious complaint which Physician cannot diagnose? The narrator tells us to be patient, but even without an explanation we sense the suggestions of imprisonment that surround Mr Merdle's 'oppressed soul', and note the inner turmoil which shows itself in the sound of 'something like a groan' when he talks of wishing to be a carpenter, his wife having rebuked him for seeming preoccupied with his business affairs. This incongruous and unhappy figure is at the centre of the society of the fashionable, wealthy and powerful in *Little Dorrit*.

Retrospective: More Mysteries (ch. 27 and others)

Throughout Book One, Dickens intersperses chapters which keep before us, and to some extent develop, two characters who first appeared at the beginning of the novel, Rigaud and Miss Wade. In chapter 16 Tattycoram confesses that the enigmatic Miss Wade, last seen in Marseilles (ch. 2), has written to her and visited her secretly, inviting her to leave the Meagles family if she feels herself 'hurt' or 'worried' and promising to look after her. At this stage Tattycoram refuses, but the incident and the suppressed anger we always see in her prepare us for the news in chapter 27 that she has at last run away from the Meagles family, infuriated by the difference between their treatment of Pet and of herself. In an attempt to retrieve Tatty, Clennam and Meagles follow her to Miss Wade's 'close, black' house in a gloomy aristocratic district. The description of the house is full of suggestions of imprisonment and impermanence which reflect Miss Wade's state of mind and refusal to accept a settled position in society.

Tatty angrily refuses to submit again to what she has experienced as humiliating treatment by the Meagles family, and we learn the cause of the emotional affinity between her and Miss Wade. Both are illegitimate and both feel wronged and angered by the disgraced position society forces upon them, a role in which they are confined by others, and from which they are unable to escape. (As illegitimacy no longer carries the stigma it did in Victorian England, we may need to remind ourselves that Dickens's fictional treatment of this theme is well founded upon fact.) Both Tatty and Miss Wade are outsiders from birth, through no fault of their own. Both are victims of a society which in effect punishes them for the misdeeds of their parents. They are 'pointed out and set apart'. Even the well-meaning Mr Meagles, as we know, has given Tattycoram a name which advertises her illegitimacy.

In one sense, chapter 27 removes some of the mystery from Miss Wade, since we can now at least partly understand her feelings and the cause of her behaviour. What remains to be resolved is what will happen to Miss Wade and to Tatty, and whether in particular Tatty, who we know is torn between love and hate for the Meagles family, has made her final choice. The Tattycoram / Miss Wade thread occupies only a small space in the novel, but it brings powerfully before us the anger of those who react to their predestined roles in the world of *Little Dorrit* with an understandably angry refusal to comply with what is forced upon them.

Another outsider with a grievance against society is Rigaud, the cosmopolitan gentleman and assassin first seen in chapter 1 leaving the Marseilles prison for what seemed like certain execution. We are probably as surprised as Cavalletto to discover in chapter 11 that Rigaud, now calling himself Lagnier, has escaped justice and is walking across France, perhaps on his way to England, still acting the gentleman. Cavalletto reappears in chapter 13, knocked down by a mail-coach in London and providentially befriended by Arthur Clennam. Rigaud, alias Lagnier, disappears until chapters 29 and 30 when he surfaces in London, now calling himself Blandois, and becomes part of the mysteries surrounding Mrs Clennam's house.

Dickens reminds us of those mysteries in occasional chapters and references which give us new information, all inconclusive. In chapter 14 we hear from Amy that Flintwinch has followed her home to the Marshalsea, and in the next chapter we see him standing up to Mrs Clennam and asking her what she intends to do for Little Dorrit. Mrs Clennam refuses to do more than employ Amy, and will not allow Flintwinch to tell her where she lives. In chapter 29, Mrs Clennam asks Amy about her family's privations, and on being told that their lives are no harder than many others, kisses her and calls her 'poor child'. All this may suggest some link between Mrs Clennam and the Dorrits, but it is impossible to be sure.

The appearance of Blandois at Mrs Clennam's, ostensibly to draw money but actually in pursuit of something else, raises further questions which are not answered. Why does he think he knows Flintwinch? Why does he insist on seeing Mrs Clennam? Why does she freely admit to him that the mysterious inscription on her late husband's watch-paper means 'Do Not Forget'? If there are family secrets, as Blandois suggests, why is she apparently unafraid to reveal them? And what are the noises we always hear in Mrs Clennam's house? All this makes perfect and instant sense once we have the key to the mystery, but its effect without that key is to bewilder us, while at the same time giving us the sense that developments are occurring which will eventually lead to a solution. All that we can be certain of is the continued confinement of Mrs Clennam, of which we are powerfully reminded. Dickens memorably compares her to her fire, which 'On rare occasions . . . flashed up passionately, as she did; but for the most part . . . was suppressed like her, and preyed upon itself evenly and slowly' (ch. 15).

Nevertheless, we know more about these mysteries than Arthur Clennam does. After hearing from Amy that Flintwinch has followed her home to the Marshalsea, Clennam learns nothing of the later developments. However, his old 'thoughts and suspicions' about his mother and Little Dorrit recur in chapters 23 and 33. His characteristic response to the news that Pancks has made a discovery about the Dorrit family is to ask whether anyone has been implicated in 'any suppression or wrong dealing of any kind' (ch. 33). Although, to his great relief, that fearful expectation is contradicted, Clennam is still left, as we are, with a sense of unsolved mystery. But these references are occasional, and in Book One Dickens alludes to the mysteries only enough to keep them in our minds while he deals with his main business of creating the wholly unmysterious themes and characters of the rest of his London world. Book One ends when Dickens has established all the main characters of the novel (with one exception, Mrs General) in their oppressive London setting, and is ready to test the Dorrit family with their unexpected accession to wealth and liberation from the Marshalsea. The last chapter of the Book contains the great set-piece scene in which Amy faints and is forgotten by her family in the pomp and excitement of their departure from the prison, an incident which reveals how little the Dorrits think about her when they believe they no longer need her.

Book the Second: Riches

Introduction: The Alps and Mrs General (chs. 1–2)

We can divide Book Two, 'Riches', into two parts. The first (chs. 1–17) develops characters and themes in preparation for the second (chs. 18–34), the lengthy climax of the novel, in which character after character comes to a crisis which marks the end of his or her part in the story. The Book begins with seven chapters set abroad and mainly concerned with the Dorrit family's new and opulent life in Italy. Chapter 1, which parallels the Marseilles chapter in Book One (also titled 'Fellow-Travellers'), takes place in the Alps and sets the events of the whole Book in perspective.

The Alpine scenery of this chapter is powerfully evoked. Our perspective moves with the travellers up from the 'fresh beauty' of the valleys where the grapes are harvested to the 'barrenness and desolation' of the high mountains. The journey, we feel, is disturbing and dangerous. Our perceptions are tricked by the changing light; distant rugged mountains at first look near and then as night falls seem to fade like ghosts. The track, which resembles 'the broken staircase of a gigantic ruin', is surrounded by images of danger and death: 'Blackened skeleton arms of wood by the wayside pointed upward to the convent, as if the ghosts of former travellers overwhelmed by the snow haunted the scene of their distress.' At the convent there is a mortuary for those travellers, who stay there for ever frozen as they were found. This awe-inspiring evocation of death amid the immensity of nature sets the day-to-day social preoccupations of the living characters in a perspective which suggests their triviality in comparison. At the same time the discomforts of the travellers in this rarefied and unfamiliar atmosphere foreshadow their social predicament in their newly elevated life in Italy.

The fellow-travellers staying at the convent are divided into two separate parties: the Dorrit family, with Mrs General; and Mr and Mrs Henry Gowan, with Blandois. Both parties have arrived by coincidence on their way to Italy, and are unknown to each other (although we discover that Amy has a letter of introduction to Pet from Arthur Clennam). By keeping their names from the reader, Dickens makes us look at them as far as possible with fresh eyes as they interact in new combinations in unfamiliar surroundings.

In the end we see that the characters behave much as we would have expected them to. Mr Dorrit, for example, has all his old pomposity mixed with a new haughtiness of manner, and still feels it his duty to play the leading role. As we see from his conversation with the monk, whose unassuming good manners contrast so favourably with the stiffness of the English travellers, Mr Dorrit's mind still runs on confinement; to him the convent feels like a kind of prison. Henry Gowan is as discordant as ever, cynically depreciating the life-saving efforts of the monks and taking so much pleasure in the sarcasm he directs at Edward Dorrit that he fails to notice that his wife has fainted. Fanny and Amy come to Pet's aid in contrasting ways; Fanny calls her servants and Amy brings water herself. Amy shows her unselfish love for Clennam by looking after the woman she thinks he loves. Blandois is as insinuating as ever, and as conspiratorial (why does he turn up near Pet's room when Amy goes to see her?). All this is done economically – every sentence contributes something to our sense of the characters – and we are left with a lively and strengthened picture of those who are to be prominent in the Italian chapters. The only new figure, Mrs General, is given a chapter of her own (ch. 2).

Dickens creates Mrs General because he needs a representative of Society to accompany the Dorrits on their grand Italian tour. Her role is to complete the education of Mr Dorrit's daughters, to fit them for the place in Society to which their new wealth entitles them. Her name suggests both something widespread and a military commanding officer. Dickens tells us that she is the widow of a 'stiff commissariat officer' devoted to 'the properties'. (For a note on the Commissariat and its insistence on the proprieties in the Crimean War, see 'A Russian War: "How not to do it" in the Crimea', in Part Three, pp. 124–9). Mrs General is also the daughter of a 'clerical dignitary', and has an adulatory testimonial from an archdeacon who has written on her behalf even though he has never set eyes on her – another example (like Bishop) of Dickens's satire on the falsity of churchmen in *Little Dorrit*. Her own humbug is neatly suggested by her interview with Mr Dorrit, in which she pretends to refuse to discuss money while making sure that she gets more from Mr Dorrit than from her previous employer.

Mrs General is an embodiment of some of the worst characteristics of Society. Her appearance is imposing, but there is nothing real behind it. She has nothing of her own to say. Her idea of education is to prevent her pupils from having opinions of their own. All she does as a teacher is teach others' views. In a striking image which suggests the mechanical, trivial, and futile training she imposes, the narrator comments: 'She had a little circular set of mental grooves or rails on which she started little trains of other people's opinions, which never overtook one another, and never got anywhere.' She denies the existence of anything improper, difficult or passionate:

> Mrs General was not to be told of anything shocking. Accidents, miseries, and offences, were never to be mentioned before her. Passion was to go to sleep in the presence of Mrs General, and blood was to change to milk and water [ch. 2].

Anything left after this formal and life-denying figure has done its worst is 'varnished' – given a glossy coat to make it look presentable.

Mrs General's attitude is the opposite of Arthur Clennam's 'I want to know'. She embodies in an extreme form a widespread ('general') tendency in Victorian England to deny the existence of anything 'improper' and to train and restrict the minds of the respectable young accordingly. As we see, Mrs General succeeds with Fanny, who after token defiance always conforms to Society's requirements, but fails with Amy, who, to her own distress and despite trying as hard as she can, is unable to force her nature into the grooves laid down by Mrs General, and so greatly disappoints her father.

The Dorrits in Italy: Riches and Freedom? (chs. 3–7 and others)

When the Dorrits are in Italy, we see least of Tip and Frederick Dorrit. Tip, now Edward Dorrit, Esquire, makes an easy transition from life in the Marshalsea to life on the Grand Tour, because, as the narrator sardonically observes, he has been well prepared by his acquaintance with horse-dealing and billiard-marking for a life spent in gambling and the other dissipations of the wealthy (ch. 5). His uncle, Frederick, also hardly seems to have changed, keeping up his old habit of carrying snuff in a piece of paper (to Fanny's annoyance), and generally showing no sign that he is aware of his good fortune, except that he stops playing the clarinet when he no longer needs to earn his living by it. He comes to life only once, with a memorable but unavailing protest against the pride and ingratitude shown in the family's treatment of Amy (ch. 5). Most of our attention is concentrated on that treatment, and on the characters of Fanny, Amy and Mr Dorrit, who are, we discover, unhappy in different ways which all reveal the shadow of the Marshalsea upon them.

Fanny is the most socially successful of the family, rapidly learning the code of manners taught her by Mrs General (we notice how quickly she picks up Mrs General's ornate and formal language), and taking advantage of her looks to become an admired young lady of great wealth. Her main motive has not changed; she is still determined to assert the family dignity, as she learned to do in the Marshalsea, and is now of course much more successful in doing so. Driven by the wish to revenge herself on Mrs Merdle, she provokes the ironically named Edmund Sparkler into renewing his suit (she is of course now eligible, since she has money). The wooing is generally treated comically (Mr Sparkler falls over in his gondola, and so on), but it has serious undertones as Fanny comes closer and closer to a loveless marriage with a man she despises, merely to take revenge on his mother and assert the family pride. Fanny's inner turmoil is seen not so much in her outward behaviour as in her confidential discussions with Amy (notably in chapter 14), when her contradictory impulses give us a strong sense of how driven she is by passions which imprison her in her past. As Amy points out, Fanny could marry someone 'very superior to Mr Sparkler', but she writhes under her sense of how Mrs Merdle has wounded the family dignity, which she feels is part of herself, and wants to seek revenge. The decision is made by the end of chapter 14, after which she makes no further admission of 'any hidden, suppressed or conquered feeling' against her marriage to a fool. But her spectacular wedding turns out to be the gateway to a 'long, long avenue of wrack and ruin' (ch. 15). Her social success is a personal disaster. And Mr Sparkler is unhappy too, wearing the 'heavy set of fetters' (ch. 6) he has put on himself.

Much the same is true of her father, who, despite his life of 'freedom and fortune', is never at ease because he can never really believe that he has left the Marshalsea behind him. No matter how deferentially he is treated, he repeatedly imagines that people know about his past in the prison and are laughing at him or insulting him. Every trivial incident becomes a major blow to his self-esteem, which depends on the pretence that he has never been poor and imprisoned for debt. The irony of all this, as we later discover, is that London Society at least knows perfectly well that he has been in the Marshalsea, but doesn't care at all as long as he now has money. But Mr Dorrit doesn't understand that, and spends his life in an agonized attempt to play the role of a wealthy gentleman who has never known disgrace and poverty.

The suffering which lies beneath this performance is revealed in chapter 5, when, while rebuking Amy for reminding him of the Marshalsea by not forming a proper ladylike surface, Mr Dorrit falls silent and then exclaims that he is 'a poor ruin and a poor wretch in the midst of his wealth'. The whole incident parallels the similar scene in Book One, chapter 19, and it shows that 'no space in the life of man could overcome that quarter of a century behind the prison bars'. For a moment, however, Mr Dorrit drops his pretences and allows Amy to show him her love. But it is only for a moment, and afterwards he resumes his life of genteel make-believe, even going so far as to plan to marry Mrs General, the epitome of social falseness, and to hand Amy over to a socially eligible husband.

Amy herself is deeply disturbed by the family's accession to wealth and their Grand Tour of Italy. Her whole life was work and looking after others, most of all her father. Now, as a lady, she is forced to be idle and can do nothing for other people, even for her father, who makes her keep her distance and expressly forbids her to show her love for him because this would detract from the family dignity. This is all the more painful to Amy as she senses – rightly, as we discover in chapter 5 – that her father is still as much in need of her love as he ever was. Dickens renders this disturbance in Little Dorrit with subtlety and power, revealing her inner feelings in her perceptions of the 'new and wonderful' world she finds in Italy, which at first seems like a dream to her because her inner life is vacant and unreal. Her memories of the prison days, when her life made sense, are more solid than her experiences in Italy, though even the Marshalsea seems 'shaken to its foundations' when she pictures it without her father.

It is characteristic of Amy in this state that of the mixed 'misery and magnificence' of Italy, the numerous beggars to whom she gives money should seem 'the only realities of the day'. Unlike Mrs General, she is certainly not ignorant of 'the existence of anything that is not perfectly proper, placid, and pleasant' in the new country around her, full of poverty and the troops of a foreign occupying power. Even at her most disturbed, Amy has a sense of reality which Mrs General and the other Dorrits lack. Instead of taking part in the 'perfect fury for making acquaintances on whom to impress their riches and importance' which seizes her family, Amy looks round Venice alone and wonders at its beauties, despite Mrs General's prohibition of wonder as ungenteel, and her particular insistence, on the authority of Mr Eustace's guide-book, that the Rialto is greatly inferior to Westminster and Blackfriars bridges. Amy is immune to the elaborate pretences which surround her in Venice, where the tourists subject themselves to a kind of mental imprisonment which resembles 'a superior sort of Marshalsea', and in Rome, where they offer themselves up like 'voluntary human sacrifices' to have their opinions formed, accepting conventional ideas rather than thinking for themselves: 'There was a formation of surface going on around her at an amazing scale, and it had not a flaw of courage or honest free speech in it' (ch. 7).

In her isolation from her family, Amy's correspondence with Arthur Clennam is very important to her, even though it is (at her request) one-sided, reflecting the inequality of their relations, and rather sad. Dickens gives two whole chapters (4 and 11) to these letters, which help to make Little Dorrit the prominent figure she is in this part of the novel, to reinforce our sense of her character, and to keep before us the idea of Amy as a lover. The letters are, of course, disguised love-letters which, like the story of the princess, subtly allow Amy to express her feelings for Clennam without revealing them directly, and they are interesting examples of how the same words can mean different things to different people.

The pretext of the letters is to keep Clennam informed of Pet's welfare, which Amy truthfully does, while minimizing the painfulness of what is obviously already an unhappy marriage. Amy's friendship with the woman Clennam loves does at least allow her some contact with Clennam, even if it causes her sadness. It also allows her to hint at her love for Clennam, while reassuring him that she will do her best for Pet: 'I will ever be as good a friend as I can for your sake.' We see in chapter 4 that her love now causes her to accept the role Clennam has forced on her, and which she used to reject, of being a 'poor child', which suggests that she has decided that any kind of relation with Clennam is better than nothing. Amy now gladly accepts from him the little he is able to give.

The gap between the two letters allows time for Amy to change, and we notice that she does. In chapter 4 she tells Clennam that she is unable to learn French and Italian. In chapter 11 she reports that she has begun to do so, inspired by Clennam's example. And we also see that by chapter 11 the beauties of Italy no longer seem unreal to her, even though they still make her think of life in the Marshalsea.

In general, Amy succeeds in Italy by avoiding the mistakes of her family. She maintains her integrity by taking no part in the elaborate and unhappy parade of pretences and falsity which make up the life of her father and sister, and by remaining true to her feelings as a lover. She alone responds to the beauties of Italian civilization in an authentically personal way. And, above all, despite her isolation and sadness, she survives the enforced end of the role of 'Little Mother', which was her

71

identity at home, and shows signs of the power to change and develop. In these ways Little Dorrit leaves the Marshalsea behind. But for the rest of her family, riches do not bring freedom.

London Again: Reminders and Developments (chs. 8–10 and others)

After the seven chapters set in Italy which begin Book Two, the action of the novel moves back to London for seven chapters (8–10, 12–13, 16–17) which remind us of various London themes and characters and help to advance the plot. Interspersed are three chapters which briefly recall us to Italy – chapter 11, Little Dorrit's second letter, and chapters 14 to 15, which are concerned with Fanny Dorrit's wedding.

Chapter 8 is set in Bleeding Heart Yard and at Twickenham. We hear that the partnership of Doyce and Clennam has prospered because Clennam has brought the financial side of the business into 'sound trim', and Doyce has continued to make inventions and improvements which have benefited the factory. We are reminded of Doyce's lack of egotism as an inventor – he 'showed the whole thing as if the Divine Artificer had made it, and he had happened to find it' – and we hear that Clennam has decided to resume the 'long and hopeless labour' of trying to persuade the Circumlocution Office, hostile as ever to those who know 'How to do it', and itself producing nothing but destruction and paperwork, of the value of Doyce's invention. We also find out that Clennam 'sadly and sorely' misses Little Dorrit, although he continues to think of her as only a 'delicate child' and of himself as too old for love. At Twickenham, Mr and Mrs Meagles decide to go to Italy to see Pet after receiving an unpleasant visit from Mrs Gowan, who maintains the usual 'genteel mystifications' about her son's marriage to Pet, and then takes the opportunity to break off relations with her social inferiors. The chapter as a whole neatly reminds us of the pretences and snobbery of London Society, and of the difficulties placed by the Barnacles in the way of those who work for the benefit of all.

Chapters 9 and 10 enmesh us again in the mysteries of the plot. As usual, what we discover does not answer the unanswered questions, but creates further mysteries. Tattycoram is seen, first at Twickenham by Mr Meagles's housekeeper (does this mean she is thinking of coming home?), and then by Arthur Clennam in London, in the company of Miss Wade and of Blandois (whom Arthur does not yet know). Acting the detective, Clennam overhears a conversation which reveals that Blandois is to be paid by Miss Wade for some service, and then follows Tattycoram and

Miss Wade to the Patriarch's house, where, comically diverted by Flora, who thinks he has come to see her, he loses them. Miss Wade's visit is, however, explained by Pancks, who reveals that the Patriarch is commissioned to pay her an allowance from an unknown source. Pancks memorably confirms our sense of Miss Wade's 'angry, passionate, reckless and revengeful' character, and says that 'she writhes under her life' – the life of someone who knows nothing of her parents or origins. In chapter 10, Clennam comes across Blandois again, this time at his mother's house, and is deeply disturbed to find that Blandois is known to his mother and Flintwinch, treats them with playful but menacing familiarity, and hints that they might wish to murder him (presumably to prevent him from revealing the family secrets).

In general, the effect of these chapters is to raise the temperature of the mysteries. Instead of trying to find out what may have happened many years before, Clennam is now confronted with something sinister undoubtedly happening in the present which links his mother with apparently dangerous characters like Blandois and Miss Wade. The unanswered questions multiply as we are left to speculate on what has brought these characters together, and whether, in particular, Miss Wade may not have been wronged by Mrs Clennam. For the next six chapters the mysteries disappear from the story (except that we are reminded of Cavalletto's fear of Blandois in chapter 13), but then a further twist is added in chapter 17 by the news that Blandois has not been seen since entering Mrs Clennam's house. The suspicion clearly is that he has been murdered there, a suspicion strengthened by the disturbing experiences of Mr Dorrit, who goes to the house to enquire about him, and, overcome by its sinister gloom, has a nightmare in which he finds 'the body of the missing Blandois, now buried in a cellar, and now bricked up in a wall'.

The increasing tension of these 'mystery' chapters is matched by developments in the public world of the novel. Chapter 12 satirically describes a 'Great Patriotic Conference', a dinner party for the Barnacles given by Mr Merdle (urged on by Mrs Merdle) so that he can provide for Edmund Sparkler on his marriage by obtaining him a post in the Circumlocution Office. In return, Mr Merdle is to help the Barnacles. This arrangement is what the Victorians called a 'job', that is, something done for private advantage under the pretence of public service.

The chapter parallels the earlier entertainment at the Merdles' (Book One, ch. 21), but its satirical tone is harsher. Mr Merdle continues to be an unimpressive figure as he oozes 'sluggishly and muddily about his drawing room', clasping himself 'by the wrists in that constabulary manner of his'. But no one cares, because he is 'immensely rich'. Dickens directs his satire not only at the worship of money, but also at the pervasive humbug of the scene – the characters pretend that they don't know what's going on, but of course they do. Bishop is a prominent target as he circulates looking 'surprisingly innocent', while playing a crucial role in getting Mr Merdle and Lord Decimus Barnacle together. The outcome is that Edmund Sparkler, described as 'thoroughly sound and practical', although everyone knows he is a fool, becomes one of the Lords of the Circumlocution Office. We also discover that Fanny's engagement to Edmund Sparkler is welcomed. Everyone knows about the history of the Dorrit family, but no one minds as long as Mr Dorrit is wealthy. This chapter completes Dickens's cynical portrayal of the ruling classes as bogus and dishonest worshippers of money. A sardonic quotation from *The Beggar's Opera* even suggests that they are no better morally than the criminals hanged at Tyburn, the former place of public execution in London.

In chapter 13, 'The Progress of an Epidemic' we follow the 'moral infection' of greed, money-worship and blind faith in Mr Merdle as it spreads through the lower and middle classes. Even in Bleeding Heart Yard those who have no money are lost in admiring deference to Mr Merdle and Edmund Sparkler. Cavalletto and Pancks have invested their savings in Mr Merdle's wonderful bank, and Pancks urges Arthur Clennam to do the same with his money, particularly as he may need a great deal to make reparation for his family's misdeeds, a powerful argument for Clennam, as we may guess. In chapter 16 Mr Dorrit catches the infection and entrusts all his money to Mr Merdle, although he notices that he looks unwell and exhausted. Throughout these chapters Dickens uses images of disease to convey his sense of how contagious and dangerous greed is. This is accompanied by allusions to Christianity which suggest that the worship of money is a kind of perverted religion. For example, in chapter 16 the excited admiration expressed for Mr Merdle – 'O, ye sun, moon and stars, the great man!' – parodies the language of the Canticle for Morning Prayer in the Church of England:

> *O ye Sun and Moon, bless ye the Lord:*
> *praise him and magnify him for ever.*
> *O ye Stars of Heaven, bless ye the Lord:*
> *praise him, and magnify him for ever.*

Having completed this picture of a nominally Christian society devoted to the worship of money, Dickens is ready for the climax of *Little Dorrit*.

Freedom at Last?

Mr Dorrit (*chs. 18–19*)

The lengthy conclusion of *Little Dorrit* occupies chapters 18–34 of Book Two. In succession the fate of the characters is decided. Pretences are dropped, the truth is revealed, the guilty are exposed, and we are able to see whether the characters escape from their oppressive and unhappy situations. First comes Mr Dorrit, whose death is powerfully described in chapters 18 and 19. Mr Dorrit predominates in these chapters (and in the preceding chapter), and for the first time in the novel his consciousness is directly rendered. This helps to give us a strong sense of his perturbed inner life, to prepare us for his death, and to make that more impressive.

Forebodings of death begin in chapter 17, in which, as we have seen, Mr Dorrit's riches and gentility do not protect him from the fear he experiences during his visit to Mrs Clennam's, which leaves him with a nightmare vision of the murder of Blandois. Then, on his journey to Rome, Mr Dorrit meets a funeral procession at night in the desolate and ruinous Campagna and feels threatened by the chanting of the priest and his gesture of salutation (we see that the menace is imagined by Mr Dorrit, as the priest's behaviour is perfectly innocent). These emotional forebodings are accompanied by a gradual physical deterioration well described by Dickens and characteristically denied by Mr Dorrit, who, with his customary self-deception, refuses to acknowledge his exhaustion and 'projects' his weakness on to his brother. Mr Dorrit's forebodings and physical deterioration add a macabre touch to his 'castle in the air', his plans for marriage with Mrs General, whom he courts successfully. This is the last act of free choice he makes, and confirms our sense of him as being determined to persist in a life of 'surface', since he seeks to attach himself to its most prominent representative.

Mr Dorrit's final decision is anticipated by two important scenes. The first, in chapter 18, is his encounter with John Chivery, which parallels and contrasts with his encounter with Mr Plornish in the Marshalsea (Book One, ch. 6). Like Mr Plornish, John Chivery well-meaningly offers Mr Dorrit cigars, as he did on a previous occasion (Book One, ch. 18). Mr Dorrit's reaction to what he experiences as a reminder of his former life in the Marshalsea is violent. He even lays hands on John Chivery, who is shocked and upset. In the end, as on the previous occasion, Mr Dorrit feels ashamed and accepts the present after all. But he has irreparably hurt Chivery's feelings, and the relationship cannot be restored. This painful scene makes us feel how friendship and good feeling are destroyed by Mr Dorrit's determination to assert his social position and to deny the past.

The second encounter is in chapter 19, when Mr Dorrit finds Amy and his brother alone together in a 'warm and bright' room. The sight reminds him of the Marshalsea and of the close relation with Amy which he has chosen to renounce so as to maintain the family's social position. He feels a pang of jealousy, which he self-deceivingly dismisses from his consciousness but expresses in querulous complaints of neglect and by sending Frederick off to bed. For the first time since his accession to wealth, Amy serves his food as she used to do, but this gives Mr Dorrit no pleasure because it reminds him of the Marshalsea, a memory he tries to thrust out of his mind by talking of his wealth and gentility. The 'undercurrents' in his voice and manner, his assertions that he can get on well without Amy and his complaint that she neglects him subtly reveal both his wish to be looked after by Amy and his inability to acknowledge this, an intolerable emotional contradiction.

From that impasse Mr Dorrit is released by his breakdown at Mrs Merdle's dinner, one of the great climactic moments of the novel. When his mind fails he believes himself back in the Marshalsea, and he addresses the aristocratic company as though they were fellow-prisoners. (There is a double irony here: the suggestion is that they really are fellow-prisoners, even if they're not in the Marshalsea, since Society is itself a prison.) Mrs Merdle is mortified by the scene – not, of course, because she doesn't know that Mr Dorrit has been in the Marshalsea, but because his experiences are being openly re-enacted. (Society must never admit to the existence of anything not 'perfectly proper, placid and pleasant', as Mrs General says in chapter 5.)

In his illness Mr Dorrit reverts for the last time to his old relationship with Amy. He loves her in his old selfish manner, allowing her to look after him just as she had in the Marshalsea, and remains contented until he dies. Death removes 'the reflected marks of the prison bars' on Mr Dorrit's face and sends him to meet his 'Father; far beyond the twilight judgement of this world; high above its mists and obscurities'. This sobering reference to eternity does not deter us or Dickens from judging that the Father of the Marshalsea never really left the prison in this world: 'his poor maimed spirit, only remembering the place where it had broken its wings, cancelled the dream through which it had since groped, and knew of nothing beyond the Marshalsea'.

Miss Wade (chs. 20–21)

In terms of the plot, Miss Wade comes back into the novel because Arthur Clennam seeks her out at Calais to make enquiries about Blandois. Chapter 20 lets us see Miss Wade living at Calais with Tattycoram, and chapter 21 is an autobiography written by Miss Wade to explain her life. The Calais setting echoes and represents Miss Wade's state of mind. The harbour is both melancholy and ferocious, and her garden is dried-up, suggesting emotional sterility. Suggestions of imprisonment are pervasive: the expatriates living at Calais remind Clennam of Marshalsea prisoners 'lounging out a limited round', and Miss Wade refers to herself as 'shut up here'. We see her cruelty as she torments Clennam with repeated reminders of how black Mrs Clennam's position looks after the mysterious disappearance of Blandois, and in her relationship with Tattycoram, 'each of the two natures . . . constantly tearing the other to pieces' (they quarrel over Tatty's visit to Twickenham, which she has concealed from Miss Wade).

Miss Wade also reveals that she hates Gowan and Pet, and gives Clennam her manuscript autobiography to explain her hatred. This indirect method of communication is in character – she is clearly unable to address herself directly to Clennam, but she does want to explain and justify her life somehow. She has presumably decided to write it for Clennam because he seems sympathetic, someone who has suffered like her, and so, unlike Mr Meagles, will be able to understand. Chapter 21 is short, but this device of letting Miss Wade tell her own story enables Dickens to give us a powerful and concentrated insight into her state of mind that would be difficult or impossible to obtain by any other means.

'The History of a Self-Tormentor' is obviously Dickens's title, not Miss Wade's. She sees her emotional history as a chronicle of ill-treatment, during which she has done nothing but defend herself against wrongs inflicted upon her. She tells the truth about her feelings and perceptions, but we can see that she is mistaken. Dickens makes it clear that she is an unreliable narrator, misunderstanding the world about her and believing that others hate her as she hates them. Unable to love or believe that others can love her, she repeatedly behaves in a way that ensures that no one does love her, hurting those about her and destroying every opportunity she has for a happy life. The only person she feels has understood her is Henry Gowan, a real tormentor, who actually does do to her what she thinks everyone else does: 'He made me feel more and more resentful, and more and more contemptible, by always presenting to me everything that surrounded me, with some new hateful light upon it, while he pretended to exhibit it in its best aspect for my admiration and his own.' Her revelation that she knows Gowan, with whom her name has never before been linked, and that she was seduced and abandoned by him ('Your dear friend amused me and amused himself as long as it suited his inclinations'), is at first a surprise, but then we can see how appropriate it is because of their emotional similarities. We can also see her emotional affinity with Tattycoram, whose 'bondage and sense of injustice' echoes Miss Wade's.

This autobiographical narrative is a remarkable fictional achievement because it makes us feel the strength of Miss Wade's passions at the same time as understanding that they are deluded. Miss Wade (her Christian name is never given, to emphasize her refusal of intimacy) is trapped in an imprisoning state of mind. Her justified bitterness over her rejection by her parents and the stigma inflicted on her as an illegitimate child has turned into a deluded and unappeasable anger which destroys love where it exists and turns life into a hateful and unforgiving battle for domination and revenge, in which she torments herself and others. After this self-exposure we can see that Miss Wade resembles Mrs Clennam, another figure imprisoned in deluded hatred, the opposite of the power of love and forgiveness represented by Little Dorrit. We can also see no way out of her suffering for Miss Wade, because she believes it is natural and inevitable. At the end of chapter 21 Miss Wade leaves us with a disturbing sense of how her character and her history have locked her in torment, a prison from which there is no escape.

Mr Merdle (*chs. 24–5*)

After Miss Wade's apologia come two linking chapters (22 and 23) which advance the plot. We hear that Doyce has been invited to work abroad for an unnamed 'barbaric Power' which values his abilities, that Clennam continues to press the Circumlocution Office to take up Doyce's invention, and that the partners have invested money in Mr Merdle's 'wonderful Bank'. Clennam also discovers from Cavalletto that Blandois is a murderer, information which deeply disturbs him, as we see from the nightmare imaginings which accompany another unavailing visit he makes to his mother's in the hope of solving the family mystery.

From Mrs Clennam's house we move in chapter 24 to the fashionable but cramped and stifling London home of Fanny and Edmund Sparkler, to find Fanny in a state of intolerable boredom on a hot summer Sunday evening. Her boredom is caused by the strain of living with her husband, aimiable as ever but no more intelligent than before, and by the frustration of being unable to move in Society because she is pregnant and her figure would show to disadvantage beside Mrs Merdle's. Everything in the scene combines to give an oppressive sense of suffocation which represents Fanny's self-inflicted fate in her unequal marriage. An unexpected visit from her father-in-law, dull and uncommunicative as ever and still 'taking himself into custody under both coat-sleeves', adds to her ill-temper. Their conversation is full of ironies which reveal Merdle's intentions. Fanny, of course, does not understand them, and we may not either on a first reading unless we know what is going to happen. But there is no mistaking the effect achieved by the remarkable device of using Fanny's consciousness to tell us something she does not herself understand. As she goes to the balcony 'for a breath of air' her eyes fill with 'waters of vexation', tears caused by her anger at the tedious company of Mrs Merdle and her husband, and they have the effect of 'making the famous Mr Merdle, in going down the street, appear to leap, and waltz, and gyrate, as if he were possessed by several Devils'. That sinister and surreal vision produced by disturbed eyesight represents Merdle's inner torment and foreshadows the disaster which is to follow.

We discover Mr Merdle's suicide through Physician, who is significantly prominent in chapter 25. Physician is important because he alone of the Society characters has no pretences: 'Where he was, something real was' (ch. 25). In his company even Mrs Merdle becomes honest and straightforward. His profession also gives him something else denied to his fashionable friends, an understanding of life's 'darkest places', which he visits doing all the good he can, showing a compassion like Christ's. It seems appropriate then that Merdle should arrange for him to be summoned after his death, and should confess to him (by letter) the secret complaint which he has never revealed in life.

Although Merdle's actual suicide is not directly described, Dickens makes the appearance of his body horrible enough to make even Physician feel 'sick and faint'. There is a grim aptness in his choice of method for his suicide – he drains his own blood away as he has drained away the economic life of the nation into unproductive and fraudulent speculation. The physical horror intensifies the moral shock of the discovery that Mr Merdle is a confidence trickster who has swindled and ruined thousands of people and has killed himself to avoid detection. Dickens ends the chapter with some bitter comments contrasting the public adulation given to Mr Merdle by 'every servile worshipper of riches' with the reality behind the myth – that he was 'the greatest Forger and the greatest Thief, that ever cheated the gallows'.

Mr Merdle's career, including his suicide, bears a marked resemblance to some financial scandals of the 1850s (for details see 'Mr Merdle's Wonderful Bank' in Part Three, pp. 131–2), and it seems probable that Dickens's contemporaries might have taken the hints of criminality which always surround Merdle rather more quickly than we may do. Nevertheless, whether or not we are expecting the revelation that Mr Merdle is a thief, there is no mistaking the stress Dickens always lays on the role his admirers and victims play in helping to create his fraudulent business empire. The greedy imaginations of the worshippers of money transform this undistinguished man into a miracle-worker and enable him to rob them. At the centre of the action of *Little Dorrit*, admired and honoured by rich and poor alike, is a confidence trickster whose victims eagerly thrust their wealth into his hands, despite his un-prepossessing appearance. In the end, inevitably, reality triumphs over illusion. Mr Merdle can only escape from his predicament at the cost of his life, and his victims are ruined.

Arthur Clennam (*chs. 26–9*)

Among those ruined by the collapse of the Merdle financial empire are the partners in Doyce and Clennam. This is the first of a series of blows to Clennam which subjects him to various tests and reduces him to a state of apparently hopeless isolation, misery and imprisonment. The chapters describing these events are tense, varied and distinguished by great subtlety in the rendering of Clennam's consciousness during this crisis in his life.

Clennam responds well to the first test, the collapse of his partnership. His own losses oppress him less than the guilt he feels for having ruined his partner by persuading him to speculate in the Merdle ventures. Characteristically, Clennam tries to atone by keeping the business going under the direction of its creditors to repay Doyce; he publicly confesses his responsibility and exonerates his partner. We see that it is entirely in keeping that the son of Mrs Clennam, who wanted to make amends for the misdeeds of his family, should honestly confess his own faults and try to make reparation. He does this in defiance of his legal adviser, Mr Rugg, who warns him to follow normal commercial practice, admit nothing and look after his own interests. But Clennam, as ever, prefers honesty to selfish prudence. However, as we might expect, this morally admirable behaviour does not impress his creditors and instead provokes animosity from the public. Clennam is arrested for debt, and, to the annoyance of Mr Rugg, chooses to enter the familiar confines of the Marshalsea (where he is assigned Mr Dorrit's old room), rather than the socially superior King's Bench prison. This is another rejection of convention which isolates and distinguishes Clennam from his fellow-citizens.

Once in the Marshalsea, Clennam is of course unable to work to repay his debts; he knows he can no longer hope to obtain his release and atone for the wrong he has done to his partner. But the hopelessness forced on him by his confinement brings with it a 'marked stop in the whirling wheel of life' which gives him time for reflection, and in chapter 27, 'The Pupil of the Marshalsea', Clennam begins to learn from his imprisonment. First, the associations of the Marshalsea naturally make him think of Little Dorrit, and in reviewing his relations with her he gradually comes to realize how much influence for good she has had upon him by setting an example of courage, patience, generosity and obedience to duty. Then Clennam hears news which feels like the shock of a 'heavy blow': John Chivery and the Plornishes tell him that Little Dorrit loves him. This surprise transforms Clennam's understanding of Amy's past behaviour. He re-reads her letters with new eyes, and re-members in particular her response (in Book One, chapter 32) when he suggested to her that she might find a lover. More important, he re-interprets his own life, seeing signs of a 'suppressed something', disguised love, in his own former thoughts and actions.

The whole scene is another remarkable example of Dickens's interest in the deeper workings of the mind, particularly the ways in which we conceal our feelings from ourselves. Clennam's sudden recognition of the truth, however surprising, is carefully prepared, as we can see if we re-read the accounts of his previous behaviour and notice there the significance which Clennam himself could not see at the time, and which we may have missed on a first reading. It is also in character that Clennam is unable to arrive at this insight by himself – he needs a stimulus from outside to overcome his inability to think consciously of Little Dorrit as anything but a kind of saintly nurse.

Even more important, and also depressingly in character, is Clennam's response to the discovery that Little Dorrit is 'the centre of the interest of his life'. He persuades himself that their opportunity for love is permanently lost, and indeed that it is better so, because Amy's love for him would have brought her back to the Marshalsea. Previously, as we know, Clennam excused his renunciation of Pet on the grounds that he was too old for love. Now we can see that his characteristic sense of defeat survives the revelation that Amy loves him despite his age. This suggests how deeply confined Clennam is in an emotional imprisonment within the walls of the Marshalsea, how he behaves as though he were once again devoid of will, purpose and hope. He is too helpless to act, or even imagine acting, on what he learns in the Marshalsea. He can no longer even dream.

As his imprisonment continues, Clennam becomes more and more isolated in the Marshalsea, and his unhappiness causes him to be rejected even by his fellow-prisoners. In this state he is confronted by two visitors who torment him in contrasting ways. One is the 'sprightly' Ferdinand Barnacle, 'very good-natured and prepossessing' as usual, who warns Clennam, in the lightest possible way, not to keep bothering the Circumlocution Office about Doyce's project when he is released, because the Office simply represents public opinion and the state of the nation, and everybody 'is ready to dislike and ridicule any invention'. He then goes on to admire Merdle as 'a master of humbug' who is bound to be followed by others who, like the Circumlocution Office, understand how to dupe the willing public. We can see that these thoughts are the worst possible ones to enter Clennam's mind, since they suggest that his efforts to influence the Circumlocution Office were bound to be futile, and that even his losses to Merdle will serve no purpose, since his fellow-citizens are happy with the present state of affairs. This adds to Clennam's sense of futility and isolation in a hostile world.

Clennam's other visitor is the gentleman murderer Blandois, found and brought by Cavalletto, who has lost his fear of his former associate now that he is no longer trying to conceal their imprisonment together. Blandois boastfully reveals that he knows Mrs Clennam's secret and is blackmailing her, dreadful news for Clennam, whose worst suspicions are confirmed at a time when he can do nothing to help or protect his mother and no longer has the power to make reparation to whomever has been wronged. Almost worse than this is Blandois's brutal but truthful taunt, which reproaches Clennam like his own conscience, that Clennam has 'sold' his friend Doyce, so confirming Blandois's view of human society as a system of mercenary betrayals. To this is added a letter from Mrs Clennam cruelly repudiating her son – 'I hope it is enough that you have ruined yourself. Rest contented without more ruin' – and Clennam is left alone with the 'haggard anxiety and remorse' which breaks his health. After a period of intense suffering, powerfully rendered through images of suffocation, Clennam lapses into delirium.

From that confusion he awakes to a sensation of something very different from the Marshalsea, the scent of 'a garden of flowers' which comes from a nosegay at his bedside. The beauty of the flowers and his intense need for them are strongly rendered by some surprising but appropriate language: 'he lifted them to his hot head, and he put them down and opened his parched hands to them, as cold hands are opened to receive the cheering of a fire'. Dickens does not describe the flowers themselves, but instead evokes their power over Clennam by combining contradictory physical sensations to make an overwhelming impression. This makes us feel, without being told, that Clennam is not so depressed that he is unable to revive; and of course the presence of flowers suggests a giver, someone who cares enough about Clennam to bring them. (We may also be reminded, by contrast, of the flowers given by Pet to Clennam in Book One, chapter 28, which he throws on the river as a symbol of renunciation, and of Clennam's lost childhood sweetheart, Flora, whose name means flower.)

The giver of the flowers is, of course, Little Dorrit, who reappears looking more womanly and showing 'the ripening touch of the Italian sun' on her face, but wearing her old dress to resume what looks like her old role in the Marshalsea, looking after Clennam this time instead of her father. Both are reluctant to talk, and when they do, we see why. Little Dorrit, admitting only to 'affection and gratitude' to Clennam, offers him her money to free him from the Marshalsea, and Clennam refuses, saying that her sacrifice would be too great. He goes on to blame himself for the 'reserve and self-mistrust' which prevented him from recognizing his love for her, and says that but for that irreparable mistake he might have been able to accept the money. Then, apparently hopelessly locked in his mental prison, Clennam embraces Amy 'as if she had been his daughter' and renounces her again, asking her not to visit him soon or often in 'this tainted place'. This leaves Clennam in 'un-utterable misery' caused by his own renewed rejection of love and help, a state of lonely and hopeless remorse, to which his character has condemned him and from which he cannot allow himself to escape. The painful chapter ends with a belated and un-Victorian declaration of 'undying love' from Little Dorrit, brought as a message by John Chivery, which in this context may seem more a gesture of despair than a sign of hope. But sign of hope it is, because Amy, undeterred by Clennam's rejection of her, at last is able to declare her feelings openly.

Mrs Clennam (*chs. 30–31*)

These exciting chapters begin with a reference to the sun's rays, striking across London, as 'bars of the prison of this lower world'. This vision is the culmination of the multiple images of confinement which pervade *Little Dorrit* – everything in this 'lower world', everything below Heaven, both within the novel and outside it, is seen as a prison.

The main incident in these chapters is Mrs Clennam's confession and self-justification, which reveals what has caused the chain of events which produced the plot of the novel and instantly clears up the mysteries of the Clennam family. It is ironical that Arthur Clennam, whose determination to find out what has happened made an essential contribution, both direct and indirect, to the solution of the family mysteries, is absent from the scene and is never allowed to find out the truth. The revelation comes first through attempted blackmail by Blandois, who torments Mrs Clennam with the gradual disclosure of her secret, and then from Mrs Clennam herself, who confesses the truth because she cannot bear to hear her life-story told by someone like Rigaud. (There is another irony here – that someone who believes that mankind is totally depraved should be so indignant when she meets a depraved individual.) Having confessed, Mrs Clennam is freed from her paralysis, which we therefore see was not a physical ailment but a psychogenic affliction, a self-imposed imprisonment, caused by guilt and unconsciously intended as a punishment for the wrong she has done to others.

The scene (it seems right to use a dramatic term) is remarkable for the increasing tension Dickens generates as we find out what Mrs Clennam has done, and why, and how it has at last come to be revealed. (There are more ironies here – her Sabbatarian refusal to destroy the incriminating document on a Sunday leads to her exposure, and Flintwinch's attempt to conceal the evidence at last brings it to light.) By the end of the chapter we can look back and understand all the mysteries and complexities of the plot (except the noises in Mrs Clennam's house), and, even more important, we have a better sense of the motives and impulses which set the plot in motion.

The family secret is that Arthur is not Mrs Clennam's son, but a love-child born to Mr Clennam and a young woman, a singer, before Mr and Mrs Clennam were married. (Mr Clennam, an orphan who had been crushed by a 'religious' upbringing, was forced into this marriage by his uncle, his guardian.) Mrs Clennam responded to this discovery with implacable hatred and rage, and sought vengeance which she justified as a religious duty. Here the narrator comments that 'no human eyes have ever seen more daring, gross, and shocking images of the Divine nature, than we creatures of the dust make in our own likenesses, of our own bad passions'. Mrs Clennam clearly has some unconscious awareness that her real motives are not those she claims: her habitual attempts to justify herself reveal inner doubts, and she makes an occasional slip of the tongue, as when she talks of herself as 'humbled and deceived' by Arthur's mother, then rapidly blushes and corrects herself, insisting that she meant that God had been injured.

Justifying herself as an instrument of divine vengeance, Mrs Clennam torments her husband, his child and the young mother, who is driven mad and locked away. And she does her best to harm even the young woman's patron, Frederick Dorrit, by withholding a legacy due to his niece, Little Dorrit. That link of course brings the Dorrits into the Clennam plot, but we should notice that Mrs Clennam is not responsible for the original imprisonment of Mr Dorrit, or for most of its continuation, since the legacy to Amy was only due on her twenty-first birthday. Dickens is not suggesting that Mrs Clennam is to blame for everything that has gone wrong in the novel. That would reduce a wide-ranging picture of an oppressive society to a simple story of domestic misdeeds. But we should realize that Mrs Clennam's justification of her hatred of Frederick Dorrit is important in the thematic structure of the novel. Frederick represents the arts because he is a musician and kept 'an idle house where singers, and players, and such-like children of Evil, turned their backs on the Light and their faces to the Darkness' and practised 'those accursed snares which are called the Arts'.

We may be surprised by the violence of the language here, but Dickens's contemporaries would not have been. It is typical of influential puritanical elements in Victorian religion and society who feared and hated the arts on religious grounds. Dickens did not need to deal with these attitudes in great detail because they were so well known. Mrs Clennam represents powerful forces in Victorian society, all associated with and justified by evangelical religion. As well as the hatred of love and imagination, there is the suspicion of childhood and the determination to give children a gloomy and miserable upbringing, the will to dominate and control, the devotion to work and acquiring money, all of which are embodied in Mrs Clennam and her prison-like 'Home', the London of *Little Dorrit*.

As we saw, Mrs Clennam's self-exposure is provoked by her determination to justify herself by telling her own story, rather than hearing it in Rigaud's version which represents her motives in an intolerable light. That confession is only partial, however, since it is not made to those she has injured, and it does not free her from the power of Rigaud, who can still blackmail her. It is his threat to sell the incriminating papers to Little Dorrit which drives Mrs Clennam to tell her story to Amy. She finds Amy in the Marshalsea, confesses the wrong she has done her, offers restitution of the withheld legacy, kneels to ask for forgiveness, and blesses Amy when she receives it. But she still continues to insist that her treatment of everyone except Amy was justified because they deserved to suffer – she was 'an instrument of severity against sin'. She asks Amy not to tell Arthur what has happened because the knowledge might wrongly destroy his picture of her as someone worthy of respect and deference. From this we can understand what the narrator meant when he comments that on her arrival at the Marshalsea she looked down into the prison 'as if it were out of her own different prison'.

Dickens takes care not to present Mrs Clennam's confession as a miraculous transformation. She is forced to confess in order to preserve her good opinion of herself. Telling her story relieves the guilt of which she is unaware, and so allows her to free herself from the wheel-chair to which she has confined herself. She can confess to Amy because she has never thought that Amy deserved punishment; she always recognized her innocence, and merely deceived herself into supposing that domestic work at the Clennam's was better for Amy than her legacy. But the essential cruelty and vindictiveness of Mrs Clennam's mental world remains as it was, still making Amy recoil with dread, and still justified as a religious duty. She makes no reply to Amy's heartfelt appeal to the New Testament, which comes with special force from a character who has just acted on its precepts:

'O, Mrs Clennam, Mrs Clennam . . . angry feelings and unforgiving deeds are no comfort and no guide to you and me . . . Be guided only by the healer of the sick, the raiser of the dead, the friend of all who were afflicted and forlorn, the patient Master who shed tears of compassion for our infirmities. We cannot but be right if we put all the rest away, and do everything in remembrance of Him. There is no vengeance and no infliction of suffering in His life, I am sure. There can be no confusion in following Him, and seeking for no other footsteps, I am certain!' (ch. 31)

This speech leads only to a tableau in which Amy's light figure standing by the window is contrasted with 'the black figure in the shade', just as Christ's life and doctrine, by which Amy lives, are in opposition to those of Mrs Clennam. The narrator sees an emblem of divine forgiveness in the tranquil radiance of the sunset, but Mrs Clennam is not impressed. This contrast between Mrs Clennam and Little Dorrit is the deepest and most important moral opposition in the novel. On the one side are anger, hatred, vengeance and the infliction of suffering, all the gloomy, life-denying and life-destroying values of the Clennam household, which make existence an oppressive state of imprisonment. On the other are love, forgiveness and freedom, not easily found in this 'prison of a lower world', but with divine power inspiring them.

The chapter ends with the long-prepared and powerfully described collapse of Mrs Clennam's house. At last we see what the noises meant – they were not ghosts or the sound of a concealed lunatic in the house, as Affery feared, and as many Victorian readers remembering *Jane Eyre* might have expected, but signs of impending structural failure. The collapse parallels the collapse of Mr Dorrit's 'castle in the air' and Mr Merdle's financial empire, and suggests the destruction of Mrs Clennam's whole way of life, as she falls with the house, permanently paralysed and silent. The collapse also crushes the unrepentant villain Rigaud, as he sits confidently waiting for the rewards of successful blackmail. Should we read this Nemesis as justified retribution for his misdeeds? If so, does that mean that Dickens does not share Little Dorrit's belief in forgiveness rather than punishment? The answer is, I think, that the novel here tests its readers by offering us the spectacle of an unpleasant character being destroyed and giving us the opportunity to examine our responses. It may be easy to feel superior to or detached from Mrs Clennam, and to give a facile assent to Little Dorrit's belief in forgiveness. The death of Rigaud may trap us into taking a delight in retribution, just like Mrs Clennam. After all, we may think he deserves what he gets. But that is what Mrs Clennam thought of her victims.

In reviewing these chapters it is natural to concentrate on the fate of Mrs Clennam. But we should not overlook two minor characters who liberate themselves from her domination in different ways. Affery at last rebels against the confusion and oppression inflicted on her by the two 'clever ones', stands up for Arthur Clennam 'when he has nothing left, and is ill and in prison, and can't stand up for himself', and insists on being told the truth. And Mr Flintwinch is revealed as someone who has enjoyed outwitting Mrs Clennam, and (unlike Rigaud) manages to make off with her money. These two escapes add to our sense that the Clennam household falls apart because it is self-defeatingly oppressive to all its inmates.

Mr Pancks and the Patriarch (*ch. 32*)

The exposure of the truth about Mrs Clennam frees Dickens to concentrate our attention on the present and future of his remaining characters. First comes the short but important chapter 32, a splendid comic scene which gives us a much-needed opportunity for laughter, as a wrongdoer is ludicrously exposed for the hypocritical cheat he is. The scene is a comic parallel and contrast to the grim death and exposure of another cheat, Mr Merdle, and although we may be grateful for the 'comic relief', we can see that it continues the theme of exposure of the guilty which pervades the last part of the novel.

The main actor is Mr Pancks, who at last rebels, provoked beyond endurance by the hypocritical extortions of his master. The imagery of steam-engines and steam-tugs which surrounds Pancks neatly suggests the intolerable pressure under which he works as a mere machine in his master's hands, and is carefully used to prepare us gradually for an explosion. This is provoked in the end by Casby's recommendation that he should dismiss his Merdle losses from his mind, stop visiting Arthur Clennam in prison, give all his attention to 'business', and squeeze the tenants of Bleeding Heart Yard harder. The immediate result is a decisive act of rebellion by Pancks which frees the tenants of Bleeding Heart Yard from their delusion that their oppressor is a venerable father to them. Pancks intercepts Casby in Bleeding Heart Yard and denounces him as a cheat and impostor worse than Merdle, and one who conceals his responsibility for his extortions by employing Pancks to do the dirty work and take the blame. Pancks then strips Casby of his patriarchal appearance by cutting off his 'sacred locks' from his head and the broad brim from his hat, so reducing him to a 'bare-polled, goggle-eyed, big-headed lumbering personage' who is left exposed to the derisive laughter of those he has cheated and misled. The chapter ends with that laughter 'rippling through the air, and making it ring again'.

Of course there is no suggestion here that the predicament of the Bleeding Hearts is suddenly abolished. They are just as poor as they ever were, and Pancks, who is now unemployed, has to make off to escape the consequences of what he has done. But nevertheless the Bleeding Hearts do at last know who keeps them 'always at it'. In this chapter mental chains are thrown away as the victims recognize their true oppressor.

Mr Meagles and Others (*ch. 33*)

In this, the second to last chapter, the plot is advanced in various ways, of which the most important is that the iron box containing the incriminating Clennam papers is recovered and placed in Amy's hands. Several characters are kept before us in preparation for the end of the novel. Little Dorrit sets about looking after Clennam every day, ignoring his request that she should only visit him occasionally, and continues to meet the selfish demands of her brother and sister. We hear that Tip has declined into drunken dependence on Amy, and Fanny remains proud and discontented, awaiting the birth of her child.

In this chapter also, three Society figures make their final appearance. Mr Sparkler keeps his place in the Circumlocution Office (there is no suggestion that the Office collapses like Mrs Clennam's house), but has an uncomfortable time of it between his wife and his mother, who continue to compete with each other. Mrs Merdle keeps her place in Society despite the death and disgrace of her husband because 'important persons' show class solidarity with her – she is treated as 'a woman of fashion and good breeding, who had been sacrificed to the wiles of a vulgar barbarian' (as Mr Merdle was recognized to be when his money ran out). Mrs General continues unemployed, despite the admiration of those who write her testimonials but do not want her themselves on any account. There are no signs of change in these characters; they remain as they were, like the Circumlocution Office and Society itself.

The main interest of the chapter, however, centres on Mr Meagles, who is seen once again in his full complexity, both good and bad. His best side is seen in his sympathy for Clennam in the Marshalsea – he feels he can't breathe properly until Clennam is released – and in the good sense and practicality which impel him to go abroad to find Daniel Doyce to help release him. We are, however, also reminded of his weaknesses, particularly in a disastrous interview with Miss Wade. Once again his limitations are revealed – he can't cope with Miss Wade as Clennam can because he can't understand her, and can't believe that she is not good-natured at heart, despite appearances. Hence his crass allusions to his daughter, and his tactless reference to Harriet as 'Tattycoram'. Miss

Wade makes her final appearance in the novel in a state of under-standable anger with Mr Meagles, whose insufferable emotional com-placency denies the reality of the feelings which dominate her life.

In contrast, however, Tattycoram is impelled by the injury Miss Wade does to Meagles by lying to him about Rigaud's iron box (the one with the incriminating Clennam papers in it) to leave her at last and return to her former master. Is this a liberation or simply a change of prisons? We can well see that life with Miss Wade, whom Tatty reliably says found 'no pleasure in anything but keeping me as miserable, suspicious, and tormenting as herself', was anything but happy. But what are we to make of Mr Meagles's reception of Tatty? He preaches her a tactless sermon on Duty, with Little Dorrit as an object-lesson. Even if we agree with the lesson, we must notice that he gives no sign of awareness that he might have failed in his own duty by treating Tattycoram so crassly that she had to run away to someone who understood and sympathized with her anger. I find it difficult to think of Tatty's flight from Miss Wade as anything more than a partial escape, from bohemian misery into bourgeois unhappiness. Tatty has learnt something, but what about Mr Meagles? He is apparently ready to resume life at Twickenham just as it used to be – except of course that his daughter is no longer there, and no longer the spoilt child but an unhappily married woman, as Mr Meagles has to recognize.

The chapter ends with Mr Meagles trying to reconcile himself to that insoluble problem. We hear that Henry Gowan, who continues to sponge on Mr Meagles's generosity, has insisted, like his mother, that he and Mr and Mrs Meagles should no longer see each other, and that Mr Meagles has agreed to this to spare Pet the sight of Gowan slighting her father in her presence. Mr Meagles tries to console himself by reflect-ing that 'she's very fond of him, and hides his faults, and thinks that no one sees them – and he certainly is well connected and of a very good family!' Here the narrator comments: 'It was the only comfort he had in the loss of his daughter, and if he made the most of it, who could blame him?' Obviously not Dickens. But we can hardly see that comfort as particularly effective, and the feeling of loss predominates, giving a sad tone to our impressions of this well-meaning character whose unchanging emotional limitations have made his daughter a 'pet' and a victim.

Amy and Arthur (*ch. 34*)

The chapter begins with a last attempt by Arthur Clennam, still weak but no longer delirious, to renounce Little Dorrit and insist that they should part when he is released from prison, as he is soon to be with the help of Daniel Doyce. Amy responds by taking the initiative, first by revealing that she has lost all her money in the Merdle swindles, and then by declaring her love openly and in effect proposing marriage – a proposal Clennam silently accepts. This reversal of the usual Victorian roles – it was the man's responsibility to make declarations and proposals – confirms our sense of Clennam as a victim in need of rescue by a heroine who, unlike him, is not burdened by guilt and lack of will, and can now act decisively to declare her love and free her lover from his compulsion to renounce her. The result is a marriage between two people who have both lost their wealth and are clearly not driven by the mercenary and social motives so apparent in the other marriages in *Little Dorrit*. But we are also left with a deepened sense of the difference between Amy's and Arthur's love. Clennam's scruples had placed a barrier between Amy and himself – he could not accept her money to release him because he could not bear to gain his liberty by depriving her of her fortune. His prospective release by Doyce and Amy's poverty remove him from that predicament, since he no longer needs the money and she no longer has it to offer. But we see that his love is affected by external circumstances in a way that Little Dorrit's is not, and that by refusing to accept money which she is willing to give, Clennam has shown an inherited belief in the importance of money which Amy does not share.

Before the wedding takes place, Clennam's partnership is restored to him by Daniel Doyce, who returns wealthy and honoured from abroad, pays his debts, forgives him for the losses he caused and reproaches him for taking them so much to heart (another character, we see, who takes the harm done by losing money less seriously than Arthur Clennam). Our final picture of the firm is completed by the news that Mr Pancks is to become first its chief clerk and later a partner.

Flora and Mr F.'s Aunt appear again, representing unrealistic romantic love and unrealistic hatred, both emotions rejected by Clennam, and Flora at last comes to terms with the loss of her childhood sweetheart – 'jealousy is not my character nor ill-will though many faults'.

Clennam chooses to stay in prison until the day of the wedding, so making a neat symbolic point: he escapes from the Marshalsea into a loving marriage, which is its opposite. Before they leave the prison together Amy arranges for Arthur to burn the incriminating codicil to the Clennam will without knowing what it is, a gesture of loving deception which marks his liberation from the inherited burdens of wrong-doing and guilt in his family's history, of which she has mercifully kept him ignorant. Their departure from the Marshalsea parallels and contrasts with the Dorrits' leaving of the prison at the end of Book One – this time there is no ostentation, and Amy is not left behind. John Chivery, on duty in the Lodge, is noticed and kindly treated by both Arthur and Amy as they leave, which reminds us of their delicacy of feeling as well as his disappointment in love. An unequivocally sad note is the absence of Mr and Mrs Meagles, who have to keep away because they would be painfully reminded of their daughter's unhappy marriage, but the wedding is otherwise quietly happy. Little Dorrit's more than nominal Christian allegiances are represented by the sun which shines on her and Arthur through 'the painted figure of Our Saviour on the window' during the ceremony.

After the signing of the register, Dickens separates Amy and Arthur from their friends, brings them out into the portico of the church and holds them there for a moment, 'looking at the fresh perspective of the street in the autumn morning sun's bright rays'. But that moment of poise and detachment is at once replaced by a closer involvement in the unglamorous reality of the street and the world before them, as they go down the steps of the church into 'a modest life of usefulness and happiness'. That life is to include, we see, looking after Fanny's neglected children (she continues to devote herself to Society) and being a 'tender nurse and friend' to the ever-selfish Tip, who dies without throwing off the shadow of the Marshalsea. Arthur and Amy disappear from our view walking together, quiet, 'inseparable and blessed'. But the last and loudest word goes to their opposites, those who surround them and are unaffected by them – 'the noisy and the eager, and the arrogant and the froward and the vain', who 'fretted, and chafed, and made their usual uproar'.

Part Two: The Pattern

The Theme and Its Treatment

Plot

Little Dorrit is a long, complex and strenuous book. Reading it can be baffling, as we are often made to recognize that we do not fully understand the fictional world Dickens has created. At the end of the story we can do what Dickens asks us to do in his Preface and consider the book as a whole, with the 'weaving' completed and the 'pattern' finished. But what is the 'pattern'?

In one sense, the intricate, and closely interwoven plot gives a structure to the novel. Characters meet and interact, one incident leads to another, and a complex chain of cause and effect leads to the dénouement, when all the plot mysteries are cleared up, and we discover what set all the events of the story in motion and what intrigues and concealments have been going on. At last we can see that the whole plot makes sense, and that Dickens has created and solved a neat and complicated puzzle, first mystifying and then enlightening us. But do we share the pleasure Dickens no doubt took in imagining this intricate plot? And does it matter if we don't?

There is no doubt that for many readers the plot of *Little Dorrit* remains baffling even after the dénouement. Not surprisingly, it is difficult to remember the complicated details. Even the useful summary of the Clennam family history given in the Penguin edition throws a light which may quickly fade as our first impressions of its mysteriousness reassert themselves. The complex interactions of the characters may cause confusion, as so many apparently unrelated figures come together in various circumstances, and characters we have grown accustomed to in one setting reappear in another. If we try drawing a diagram to represent the interactions and relations between characters, it soon becomes intolerably complicated. Even if we can remember the details of the plot, that in itself may not give us a clear sense of the pattern of the story – we may merely be left with a bewildering impression of interconnected characters and incidents which have no meaning. And there is also a danger that if we think too long about the plot we may become impatient of the coincidences on which it often depends.

The best way out of this impasse, I would suggest, is to leave the plot to those who can follow and enjoy it, and to look elsewhere for the pattern of *Little Dorrit*. That pattern is best seen in the central theme of the book, which gives the plot its true significance.

Theme and Variations

In its structure, *Little Dorrit* resembles other major nineteenth-century novels. At the beginning a central theme is dramatically stated, embodied in characters, incidents and setting, and then developed and varied in contrasting but related areas. The 'pattern' of *Little Dorrit* can be clearly seen when we perceive that central theme and follow it through all its ramifications and developments. If we do that, then the complexities of the plot cease to baffle and we no longer share the bewilderment of some of the characters in the story. The central theme pervades the major and minor characters, incidents, institutions and settings of the novel, all of which are related to the main idea and make sense in terms of the whole. This method allows Dickens to give cohesion to a very long, diverse and wide-ranging narrative, as he concentrates on whatever is relevant to his main theme and excludes from the story anything that is not.

The central theme of *Little Dorrit*, stated in chapter 1 and developed throughout the book, is usually said to be 'imprisonment', but 'confinement and freedom' would be more precise. There are of course real and important prisons in the fictional world of *Little Dorrit*, but the story is certainly not limited to those. Dickens is also concerned with individuals and groups whose state of mind or social position feels like a prison, and who are thwarted, oppressed and damaged by others and even by themselves. *Little Dorrit* depicts a prison-world in which life is generally oppressive, and even those who are nominally free are in fact confined. Places, institutions, classes, families and individuals combine to create a picture of England as one large prison with many cells. The novel also explores how that prison-world is maintained, and how it can be escaped.

The settings of *Little Dorrit* are remorselessly prison-like. The story begins abroad, in a criminal prison in Marseilles, and then moves to the place in that city where travellers are kept in quarantine to see if they develop diseases. The expatriates at Calais look like Marshalsea prisoners, and Miss Wade's house there is oppressive. The inn at Chalons becomes a trap for Cavalletto, the innocent traveller, when his criminal associate Rigaud unexpectedly catches up with him. The convent at the

Great St Bernard Pass feels like a prison. Italy is occupied and oppressed by foreign troops. The expatriates in Venice and Rome behave as though they were in a jail. There is no relief or escape abroad (except for Daniel Doyce, in countries we never see) from oppression at home. In England, there are only two settings outside London, both close to it. Hampton Court is a red-brick dungeon for its discontented inhabitants, and Mr Meagles's apparently peaceful house in the country at Twickenham is painful to its occupants and visitors.

The story is, however, dominated by London, a city repeatedly described in images of decay, oppression, gloom, disease and death. Mrs Clennam's house is ramshackle, dark and tormented. The Marshalsea prison stifles its inmates. The poor wander the streets in the cold and rain or live, oppressed and exploited, in Bleeding Heart Yard. Their extortionate landlord, Mr Casby, lives in another prison-like house. Other wealthy people – Mr Barnacle, Mr Merdle, Mr and Mrs Sparkler – live in stifling and gloomy houses in respectable districts. All these settings reflect and embody the lives of the people who live in them. All are powerfully evoked in language which is varied enough to create interesting differences between the settings, and consistent enough to offer no escape from the prevailing mood of confinement.

The institutions which appear in these settings are all oppressive and damaging. The prisons, both criminal and civil, confine their inmates, as we would expect, but they are also microcosms of a society which thwarts and damages its members. Of the prisons in Victorian London, only the Marshalsea appears in *Little Dorrit*. (Another debtors' prison, the King's Bench, is mentioned in passing.) Dickens concentrates on debt and imprisonment for debt, a punishment which, as we have seen, prevents the debtor from working to liberate himself, and may confine him for life. This appalling retribution suggests how seriously money and the failure to pay debts are taken – other obligations are flouted with impunity in *Little Dorrit*. Another representative and dominant institution is the Circumlocution Office, an instrument of government which paralyses the whole nation by thwarting and obstructing anyone or anything useful, beneficial or creative. The Circumlocution Office is a family business, controlled in their own interests by the Barnacles, a group of aristocratic parasites. Away from the office the Barnacles amuse themselves in Society, a stagnant, hypocritical and superficial parade of materialism. Linked to Society is another kind of institution represented by Mr Merdle, the swindler whose financial empire receives the deference and admiration of his fellow-citizens, who worship money and are ruined by him.

The same atmosphere of confinement and damage is also found in the families which appear in *Little Dorrit*, although they have different places in society and are unhappy in different ways. For example, the Plornish family, who represent the poor, are trapped in Bleeding Heart Yard, either unemployed or overworked but always in poverty, struggling to keep alive. Mr Plornish's father has to go into confinement in the workhouse because they can't afford to keep him. However, most families in *Little Dorrit* are middle-class and connected in some way with commerce: the Clennams, the Meagleses, the Dorrits and the Casbys. The parents in these families are inadequate or destructive, and their children damaged in different ways. Mrs Clennam has inflicted a cruel upbringing on her supposed son, Arthur, and has deprived him of will, purpose and hope. Mr Meagles, in contrast, has spoiled his daughter and brought her up to be a 'Pet'. Mr Dorrit's inadequacy lands him and his children in the Marshalsea, where they grow up with the shadow of its walls upon them. Mr Casby pretends to be a 'Patriarch', an ideal father, to his large 'family' of tenants, but in fact oppresses them.

The marriages in these families are likewise generally loveless and unhappy. Mr Merdle's relations with his wife are purely formal. The marriage of Mr and Mrs Clennam, forced upon them by the older generation, was full of hatred and aversion, and the girl whom Mr Clennam loved was abandoned and driven mad. Mrs Flintwinch is also forced into a loveless marriage for the convenience of her employer and a fellow-servant. The marriage of Mr and Mrs Meagles is damaged when their daughter marries an unloving man. The lively and attractive Fanny Dorrit marries the brainless Edmund Sparkler to revenge herself on his mother, and feels trapped in endless boredom. And there is no relief from this generally unhappy picture of families, parenthood and marriage to be found among the characters who are excluded from conventional family relations by unorthodox sexual behaviour or illegitimacy. The prostitute who accosts Amy and Maggy during their nocturnal 'party' on the London streets (Book One, ch. 14) is suicidally distraught, and Tattycoram has to choose between an intolerable life as a servant of the Meagles family or an intolerable life as a companion to Miss Wade, the self-tormentor.

Miss Wade, who lives a life of obsessed hatred, is typical of the many unhappy individuals in *Little Dorrit* who are confined and damaged, usually by their own temperaments and by their social role. Mr Merdle is obsessed by his mysterious 'complaint', wears imaginary handcuffs amid his wealth and prestige, and lives a miserable life in his mansion under the disapproving eye of the Chief Butler. Henry Gowan and his mother are both trapped in their grievance against their relatives, who do not do enough to provide for them. Mrs Clennam distorts Christianity in the service of her own bad passions, and imprisons herself in her room in guilt-induced paralysis. Mr Dorrit can never escape the role he created for himself as Father of the Marshalsea, and nothing essential changes when he is released from prison. Mr Meagles can never escape his emotional limitations. Maggy is condemned to a perpetual and unchanging childhood by disease, and Pancks is forced to act as Casby's 'grinder', like a machine. Even characters like Amy and Arthur who try to free themselves from the constrictions of upbringing and temperament are to some extent damaged. And Daniel Doyce, the only character in the novel whose inner life is untainted by the prison-world, can only work freely and receive the recognition and rewards he deserves abroad.

These imprisoned figures are characteristically solitary and unhappy. *Little Dorrit* is full of characters who lead lonely and isolated lives. Sometimes the isolation is obvious, as in the cases of Mrs Clennam and Miss Wade, who ostentatiously cut themselves off from society, or of Mr Dorrit, who is forced into prison. Others, like Mr Merdle, are isolated in a crowd. Amy Dorrit spends most of the book in a state of hopeless love which she cannot reveal to others. And Arthur Clennam, whose consciousness is so prominent in the story, feels irretrievably lonely. There is a great deal of solitary confinement in the prison-world of *Little Dorrit*, and much suffering, not only from the inner misery of imprisoned states of mind, but in the cruel, selfish and exploiting relationships which pervade the book. The cruelty of its main institutions, the Circumlocution Office and the Marshalsea, is echoed in the relations between characters, in which so often the strong oppress and damage the weak. Flintwinch, Mrs Clennam, Gowan, Rigaud, Casby and Mr Dorrit in different ways batten on those whose wills are less determined than theirs, and do them harm. Some of these victimizers, for example Casby, lead contented lives amid the misery which surrounds them, and which they have caused, but others, like Mrs Clennam and Mr Dorrit, suffer like their victims. The self-tormentors torment others as well as themselves. The characters of *Little Dorrit* are jailers or captives, sometimes both at the same time, and the world they live in is a suffocating prison.

What Preserves the Prison-World?

How do the figures who live in the prison-world of *Little Dorrit* respond to their captivity? Their usual reaction is to attempt to deny reality and so conceal the intolerable truth from themselves and from others. Most characters in *Little Dorrit* create fictions about themselves, their position in society, their relations with others and the world they live in. They then live by these fictions, which are occasionally harmless but usually damaging because the intricate deceptions and pretences they involve imprison their authors still further. And yet at the same time such fictions may reveal truths about the characters and the world they live in which they would prefer to conceal.

The most terrible of these self-confined characters are Miss Wade, Mrs Clennam and Mr Dorrit. Miss Wade's determined belief that others despise her allows her to see herself only as an innocent victim and to deny her own share of the responsibility for her predicament. At the same time, these delusions which imprison her permanently are only partial; she does in fact suffer the stigma of an illegitimate birth for which she is in no way responsible, and for which society nevertheless punishes her. Mrs Clennam deceives herself into believing that her anger, jealousy, and hatred are divinely inspired virtues, and that her revenge is an expression of divine justice. She also sanctifies her commercialism as a religious impulse. And yet these attempts to whitewash her motives do not convince even Mrs Clennam herself. Without conscious recognition of what she is doing, she confines herself in a wheel-chair as punishment for the wrongs she has inflicted on others.

This exposure of a cruel character who is deeply at odds with herself and unable to face the truth about her motives also exposes the ruthless and sanctimonious commercial society to which she belongs and of which she is partly typical. We are led to see the oppressive London of *Little Dorrit* as a creation or reflection of imprisoned and imprisoning minds like Mrs Clennam's, a larger version of the horrible life she creates for herself in her own house and inflicts on her adopted son. In contrast to Mrs Clennam, Arthur generally sees the world he lives in as it is, but he also creates damaging fictions, such as his almost incorrigible belief that he is too old and Little Dorrit too young for love. And he too shares the common belief in the power of money in the world of *Little Dorrit* when he refuses to allow Amy to free him from the Marshalsea by giving him her fortune – as though money were more important than love.

The most remarkable self-deceiver in the book is Mr Dorrit, whose uneasy attempts to impose on himself and others are treated with consistent subtlety. In an understandable but disastrous attempt to protect himself from the suffocating horror of an indefinite and hopeless imprisonment for reasons he cannot even understand, Mr Dorrit adapts himself to prison life by creating a role as Father of the Marshalsea. This allows him to assert the family gentility, which is confirmed by his fierce pretence that his children do not work to support themselves and him, and his insistence that the beggar's alms he receives are 'testimonials' to his exalted position. These pretences are no more convincing than the attempts by other prisoners to delude themselves, for example the well-adapted and wholly defeated jail-birds who believe that they have found true freedom in prison. But Mr Dorrit's self-created prison prevents him from ever escaping confinement; his new world of wealth and freedom turns out no better than the Marshalsea. Mr Dorrit's devotion to his image of himself as a gentleman who does no work and is therefore rewarded by the esteem and deference of others helps to expose idle gentility for what it is in the story – a parasitic confidence trick.

Pretences of a similar kind pervade Society in *Little Dorrit*, which conceals its prime interest in money under various veneers. Mrs Gowan pretends and asserts that her son has fallen victim to Pet's beauty because Mr and Mrs Meagles have been scheming to raise their social standing by achieving a genteel marriage for her. The fiction is untrue – we know that Pet's parents have opposed the match – but it reminds us of Mr Meagles's unfortunate and all too genuine deference to rank and family. This deference is untouched by his knowledge of what the Circumlocution Office, which exists solely to protect the privileged and exploiting position of the aristocratic Barnacles, has done to Daniel Doyce. The engaging Ferdinand Barnacle admits that the Office is a gigantic sham and explains its persistence despite the damage it does as a consequence of the public's readiness to be cheated, its preference for the bogus and the fake. This preference shows itself not only in Mr Meagles, but in the Bleeding Hearts, with their belief in the Barnacles and in Mr Casby, the exploiter who passes for a benign father-figure.

Similar pretences to Casby's are found in Mr Merdle, the swindler who passes for a public benefactor and hero. This deception inflicts a miserable life and death on Mr Merdle, as well as ruin on his victims, but his enormous and easy success, despite his unprepossessing and indeed criminal appearance, shows how ready the public is, from Barnacles, Bar and Bishop downwards to the Bleeding Hearts, to defer to wealth and to imagine that it can be effortlessly obtained. Society's pretences are perhaps most clearly represented in Mrs General, who embodies in an extreme form the widespread tendency to pretend that the disagreeable does not exist, and to 'varnish' what cannot be concealed. As she is a character with no depth, we could hardly say that Mrs General traps and damages herself with these pretences, but she does achieve the opposite of what she intends, since her efforts at suppression only remind us of what is being concealed.

We may in contrast welcome the cynical admissions of exceptional characters such as Ferdinand Barnacle, Henry Gowan and Rigaud, who confess the truths which the self-deceptions of others attempt to conceal. Henry Gowan traps himself in his genteel grievance against the world which has not given him the easy money he believes his birth entitles him to, and he does not escape his chosen role as cynical and destructive underminer of the beautiful and the good. But he does tell the truth about Society in *Little Dorrit*, a market-place for cheats who make money by passing off the sham for the real – 'so great the success, so great the imposition' (Book One, ch. 26) – even while he joins in the cheating. So too does Rigaud, who in pursuing without scruple what he thinks are his own interests, and revenging himself on a society which has not treated him as he also believes he deserves, declares that, like everyone else, he lives by his wits and sells 'anything that commands a price' (Book Two, ch. 28).

These characters who openly confess the gentlemanly confidence tricks by which they live contrast sharply with most of the captives in the prison-world of *Little Dorrit* who strongly prefer comfortable delusions to seeing the world they live in as it really is. But neither those who confess their deceptions of others nor those who take refuge in deceiving themselves escape confinement.

Who Escapes?

In the title-page illustration to the novel half the title is printed in chains, but the other half – the 'Little' – is free. Are we then to suppose that many characters are unaffected by the prison-world, or escape from it? There is certainly no liberating institution in the story to match the Marshalsea and the Circumlocution Office, and some of the possible means of escape, such as religion, love and art, turn into bars of the prison. Institutional religion, for example, is represented by Bishop, who worships Mr Merdle, and by Mrs Clennam, whose hate-filled fantasies help to produce the gloomy commercialism of London. Love is often replaced by hatred or the mercenary and social motives which dominate marriage in the story. And art, which might have allowed people the free and happy use of their imaginations and the opportunity to criticize the society to which they belong, is generally crushed or perverted in the world of *Little Dorrit*.

We can see this frustration of the creative imagination exemplified in character after character in the novel. Arthur Clennam's mother, the singer, is deprived of happiness and driven mad, and Frederick Dorrit turns from a cultivated patron into a professional musician who plays mechanically for a living, without enjoyment, fates which gratify Mrs Clennam's representative hatred of the arts. In Society, art is emptied of its significance by the Barnacles, who convert it into a meaningless, snobbish sham. The representative Society artist is Henry Gowan, the gentlemanly amateur and cynical underminer of art and morality who recognizes his own fraudulence but insists that all artists are the same. Gowan fits well into a milieu in which the connoisseurs are represented by Mr Meagles, who has amassed a comic collection of highly regarded rubbish on his travels, and by Mrs General, who does her best to destroy wonder at the beauties of Italy. The only artistic characters in *Little Dorrit* who escape these blights are Cavalletto and Doyce. Cavalletto carves in wood and is able to sell what he has made, and Doyce continues to invent despite all discouragements. But Cavalletto is an exotic import who contrasts with the natives of Bleeding Heart Yard, and Doyce can only make full use of his creative powers abroad.

At the end of the story, there is no radical transformation of the prison-world. Mrs Clennam's house may collapse, but London as a whole is unchanged, and Society, the Circumlocution Office and the Marshalsea carry on as before. No doubt it would hardly be plausible if *Little Dorrit* ended with a sudden great escape from the prison. We have seen too many characters like Mr Dorrit helping to create that prison and locking themselves into it. But there is one general trend towards the end of the novel. Pretences and concealments of all kinds are stripped away, the guilty are exposed and the truth is revealed in various contrasting ways which all suggest that the great edifice of humbug, sham and lies in *Little Dorrit* is too unstable to last.

It would, however, be wrong to conclude that the abandonment of pretence in itself means a general casting off of chains. Miss Wade, for example, at last reveals the truth as she sees it about her extraordinary behaviour, but her disclosure only convinces us that she is hopelessly trapped by her delusions. Mr Dorrit breaks down and abandons the arduous pretences of his opulent life in Italy, but reverts in his imagination to the Marshalsea, which he has never really left, and dies. Mr Merdle frees himself from the tension and misery of pretending to be a public benefactor, and his financial empire is exposed as a sham, but he escapes only by suicide. Arthur Clennam at least recognizes the truth about his love for Amy and her love for him, but locks himself firmly in a mental prison by renouncing love and marriage. Mrs Clennam is at last forced to tell the truth about what she has done, and is able to leave her wheelchair and ask one of her victims for forgiveness. But she achieves no insight into the cruelty of her motives, and falls silent as her house collapses, still persuaded that with the exception of her treatment of Little Dorrit, she has acted in the interests of true religion. Other characters show no signs of change, despite the upheavals around them, but carry on in their appointed cells as before. The Society figures, Mrs Merdle, Mrs General and Mrs Sparkler, make no response to the collapse of Mr Merdle and Mr Dorrit other than to behave as they have always done. Mr Meagles continues to love a lord and learns nothing from the loss and return of Tattycoram.

Some characters do show signs of a new freedom, but their liberation is qualified. Pancks frees himself from his intolerable role as his master's grinder, and exposes Casby to his tenants as the hypocritical exploiter he is, but we are not to suppose that denunciation alone can bring prosperity to Bleeding Heart Yard. Mr Flintwinch escapes abroad, but only as a thief. Mrs Flintwinch does liberate herself from her overbearing husband and employer, but she is only a minor character. There is little in the dénouement of *Little Dorrit* to suggest that the prison walls are crumbling, and if we exclude the love and marriage of Arthur and Amy, little to add to our previous impression that only a few characters maintain a precarious and limited freedom in the prison-world. Cavalletto, as always, is an outsider immune from the gloom of Bleeding Heart Yard, and he is at last freed from his fear of Blandois when he no longer has to conceal his former association with him, and Doyce, as always, does not allow the prison to enter his soul. There seems to be hope for these men and their associates, but it is not a new hope which suddenly appears at the end of the novel.

If we are to see new hope at the end of *Little Dorrit*, it must be in the marriage of Amy and Arthur, the nearest thing to a happy ending that the story allows. Little Dorrit, who has always been the major character least affected by pretences and delusions, concludes the story by forgiving Mrs Clennam and rescuing her adopted son from his self-inflicted mental imprisonment. Amy lives by a New Testament religion of peace and forgiveness which contrasts with and at last replaces in the story Mrs Clennam's devotion to hatred and vengeance. Dickens does not flinch from depicting the likely fate of the meek in the world of *Little Dorrit*; we have seen Amy's selfless love exploited by her family. At the end of the story she marries someone, who, like her father, is a Marshalsea prisoner and a victim of the prison-world in *Little Dorrit*, but who, unlike Mr Dorrit, is a reflective, responsible and unselfish character, sensitive to the feelings of others. This is an unequivocally happy ending for Clennam, who at last escapes his dreadful upbringing and leaves the Marshalsea for a loving marriage brought to him by the greater love and strength of character of Little Dorrit. The author does not mean us to imagine that Clennam could emancipate himself from the shadow of the woman he continues to think of as his mother, and we notice that Dickens conveys a sense of fragility in Clennam by making Amy decide that he should never find out the painful truth about his family history.

Clennam, who began devoid of will, purpose and hope, finds love with Little Dorrit and fulfilling work with his business partners to replace the gloomy hatreds and obsessed commercialism of his family. Amy rescues a devoted man who has every reason to love her, and who does not exploit her, though he certainly needs her. But her marriage brings no miraculous transformation of her life: she continues to look after her scapegrace brother, and her sister's neglected children – a new generation of victims damaged by their mother's continuing obsession with Society. And the last paragraphs of the novel associate Amy's and Arthur's 'modest life of usefulness and happiness' with reminders of neglect, futility and death, and surround their 'inseparable and blessed' marriage with 'the noisy and the eager, and the arrogant and the froward and the vain', who 'fretted and chafed, and made their usual uproar'. Their quietly happy love makes no difference to the greater world around them, which continues as before.

Readers respond to the conclusion of *Little Dorrit* in different ways. Some, the optimistic, find it a kind of triumph (admittedly a rather sombre triumph), as the child of the Marshalsea and the child of Mrs Clennam survive everything that is done to them and at last achieve a joyful serenity unspoilt by the hostile and uncomprehending society around them. Others, the pessimists, stress how hard-won and limited their achievement is, and how it is almost extinguished by the over-whelming weight of the hostile world. These are both partial responses, however, because the ending keeps both the love and the uproar alive.

Dickens does not use the ending to obliterate either Little Dorrit or her opposites. The novel stops as it began and as it continued, with the opposing forces both present and both strongly created. At the end the conflict is left permanently unresolved. Dickens avoids both the sentimentality which might have concentrated on the marriage of Amy and Arthur, forgetting the prison-world around them, and the pessimism which might have ended the story with an unchanged prison-world and no 'modest life of usefulness and happiness' within it. This leads me to a general point. If we wish to decide how pessimistic or optimistic *Little Dorrit* is, we should not simply immerse ourselves in the imaginary world Dickens creates and work out who escapes from the prison and who remains trapped. We should also consider Dickens's art.

Dickens's Art

In *Little Dorrit* Dickens depicts England as a prison. His vision is systematic and complete. A few characters partly or belatedly escape the prison walls, but for most the England of *Little Dorrit* is a suffocating country which confines and damages those who live in it. Places, institutions, religion, attitudes, social classes, families and individuals are all part of the prison-world, as we have seen. What relation does this fictional world bear to the England of the 1850s? And should our impression of the book be preponderantly gloomy? In Part Three I discuss some of *Little Dorrit*'s context in the light of Dickens's defence of the book and of historical evidence of various kinds. For the moment, remembering that the story can be appreciated by those who know nothing of mid-Victorian history, I would like to make a point which depends more on logic than on knowledge of the past. If England in 1855 had been no more than the England of *Little Dorrit*, then *Little Dorrit* could not have been written. In the world of the novel, as we have seen, art is exiled, crushed or trivialized. But in 1855, in the real world, Dickens's art was very much alive, and he was the most popular novelist of the age (see Part Three). The great countervailing force to the pressure of imprisonment in *Little Dorrit* is the liberating art of Charles Dickens which created the novel and which pervades it.

Like other Victorian novelists, Dickens had the confidence, the audacity and the energy to write novels which attempted to grasp and analyse a whole society, to portray its social classes, its institutions, its religion, its habits of thought and behaviour. Victorian novelists occupied territory which is now the province of various specialists, such as sociologists and psychologists. They could be moralists who used their fiction to alert, warn, encourage and perhaps transform their fellow-citizens. And to do that they wrote fiction which gave pleasure, and so affirmed the power of art against those who distrusted or trivialized it. In *Little Dorrit* Dickens chooses to create a vision of Victorian England as a prison which crushes and blights its inmates. But in creating that vision he wrote for readers who are not trapped in the prison which the novel describes. Dickens shows confidence that his readers can face and understand some of the worst tendencies in Victorian England and in human nature, and can take pleasure in a work of art which defies those tendencies.

In *Little Dorrit*, Dickens pays implicit tribute to the courage of his readers. He makes us imagine an England which is intolerably oppressive. We share the unglamorous, humiliating and restricted life of the inmates. There is nothing exciting or conventionally heroic – the hero is a depressed middle-aged man and the heroine an oppressed and exploited young woman. The characters live in a society which cages and harms them. They damage each other, and themselves. The pervading tone of the book is of suffering and defeat. Everything contributes to the overwhelmingly oppressive atmosphere. We are expected to share the bewildered suffering of the inmates of the fictional prison, and we are not allowed to take refuge in the evasions and pretences which the characters employ to defend themselves against the world they live in. Unlike Mrs General, we do not avoid the disagreeable. The narrator reminds us that the faults of the characters are our faults too. (For example, see Book One, chapters 13 and 17, for comments on Clennam's self-deception and Meagles's snobbery.) The pretences of the characters are ruthlessly stripped away and the reader is allowed no wish-fulfilling fictional consolations. Amy Dorrit suffers because she is good and can be exploited. Mr Dorrit suddenly inherits great wealth and is freed from the Marshalsea, but never finds real freedom or happiness. There is no poetic justice to reverse the destinies the characters create for themselves. And there is no conventional happy ending to blur the effect of the rest of the book.

Implicit in this gloomy fictional world is Dickens's belief that his readers have the courage to understand and share this systematic depiction of characters whose lives and destinies are in many ways the worst that could be imagined, trapped in a prison which they cannot bear to face and so have not the strength to change. Dickens assumes and implies that his readers are different, with the courage to understand the forces which defeat his characters. In this way, *Little Dorrit* becomes a tragic book, even though none of its characters has the stature of a tragic hero, because it looks unflinchingly at some of the worst possibilities of human life and implies that we have the strength to face them. That in itself defies the imprisoning forces which overwhelm most of the characters in *Little Dorrit* and damage them all.

Dickens's respect for his readers can also be seen in other aspects of the novel. We are expected to follow an intricate plot which helps to unify his vision of an imprisoned world, and to trace the central theme as it is developed in a long and complex work. Dickens often presents us with choices, problems and dilemmas, as well as the assured authorial guidance usually found in Victorian fiction. Sometimes the narrator intervenes to direct our responses to a character or incident, but often, as we have seen, at the most crucial moments he is silent, and Dickens leaves us to work out our own view of what is happening. In this way we are given the opportunity to take an independent view, without interference from the author.

Dickens also subtly challenges conventional attitudes by setting them in a particular literary context, without comment. For example, duty was a highly regarded virtue in Victorian England, but Dickens puts a conventional and complacent tribute to it in the mouth of Mr Meagles, a character who has no understanding of how intolerably oppressive the dutiful life can be, and so unintentionally undermines the values he wishes to commend (Book Two, ch. 33). And we are expected to take the force of sharp comments wherever they come from. It is the liar Rigaud who casts a shrewd light on the self-deceptions of others when he asks whether all those who wish to tear him apart for murdering his wife are on good terms with their own (Book One, ch. 11).

To all this Dickens adds a subtlety of characterization which requires sensitive collaboration from the reader, and which can give great pleasure. This is based on a sharp and unconventional perception of human behaviour. For example, his description of Maggy (Book One, ch. 9) refers to her 'unnaturally still' eyes, which are 'very little affected by light'. The distinguished neurologist Russell Brain points out in *Some Reflections on Genius* (1960) that this describes what is now known as the Argyll Robertson pupil, a sign of the damage done by disease which the medical profession had not recognized in Dickens's time but which Dickens saw and understood. As usual in his work, the precise physical detail signifies something beyond itself. Dickens reveals the inner lives of his characters and expresses their feelings not only by his occasional direct rendering of their consciousnesses, but also through their gestures and appearances, and the settings in which they live. This is particularly appropriate and successful in *Little Dorrit* because so many of the characters are inarticulate, lack self-knowledge or make a practice of deceiving themselves. Mr Dorrit's consciousness, for example, is not directly rendered until just before his death, and until then we have the satisfaction of noticing how he betrays his true feelings whenever his elaborate system of pretences breaks down under stress.

This method of characterization allows us room to make up our own minds, and to work with Dickens as an acknowledged collaborator in the creation of a fictional world. As we are rarely given privileged insight into a character's mind, the effect is to strengthen our confidence in our own perceptions and imagination. And when Dickens's authorial presence does become prominent in a character description, he often relies on witty and enjoyable methods. For example, he crystallizes our impression of Mrs General in Italy by describing her 'scratching up the driest little bones of antiquity, and bolting them whole without any human visitings – like a Ghoule in gloves' (Book Two, ch. 16). This combination of metaphor and simile allows us to share Dickens's delight in the alliterative word-play of 'Ghoule in gloves', which undermines Mrs General's genteel pretensions by linking them with a macabre image which suggests how deadly they are.

Dickens's humour is important but certainly not predominant in *Little Dorrit*. It is seldom discussed, perhaps because analysing laughter reminds us too much of the dismal experience of trying to explain a joke to someone who has missed its point. But humour makes a vital contribution to the complete effect of *Little Dorrit*. The jokes are always relevant to the sombre central themes of the novel, but they provide a valuable intrusion of cheerfulness and give us a welcome opportunity to laugh at what often seems too grim to be borne. For example, Mrs General's 'prunes and prisms' helps to make her affected formation of surface ludicrous as well as sinister and destructive. The comic episode of Plornish's negotiations with the supposed Captain Maroon for the release of Tip (Book One, ch. 13) treats important themes of the novel (pretences, and the settlement of debts) in a pleasantly jocular fashion which temporarily relieves the gloom of Bleeding Heart Yard. Mr Pancks's appearance and the inner tensions it reveals are always described humorously to prepare us for his assault on Casby, which inflicts comic justice on the old hypocrite by revealing him for what he is to his victims, a discovery they celebrate with an explosion of laughter. Most important of the comic characters is Flora Finching, whose exuberant comic absurdity mixed with honesty and good feeling contributes such a vital ingredient to the *Little Dorrit* mixture. Once Flora has described Mrs Clennam as 'glowering at me like Fate in a go-cart' (Book One, ch. 24), Mrs Clennam never seems quite so menacing again.

Since it is difficult to sympathize with characters we laugh at, Dickens is careful with his humour in the presence of figures such as Arthur Clennam and Mr Dorrit. But even here it contributes to some of his most memorable effects, such as Clennam's repeated embarrassment as the middle-aged Flora re-enacts the romantic passion of her youth, and the laughter (among other feelings) provoked by Mr Dorrit's patronage of old Mr Nandy (Book One, ch. 31). In general, whenever the comic spirit is found in *Little Dorrit* (and it is often heard in Dickens's language), it brings liberation from the prison-world by implying that those who laugh are sane, cheerful, and free.

Language is, of course, the medium of *Little Dorrit*, and everything Dickens achieves depends on his use of English (although the illustrations can certainly contribute to our sense of the book). In general, the inexhaustible vitality of Dickens's language contrasts sharply with the depressed prison-world it creates in *Little Dorrit*. The effect is to undermine that prison-world with the energy, vivacity and playful freedom of an artist who is not trapped in the imprisoning states of mind which confine the characters he creates. Dickens's language embodies qualities which are the antithesis of the gloomy, obsessed and pretentious world of the novel. When for example he writes that 'Mrs Merdle concurred with all her heart – or with all her art, which was exactly the same thing' (Book Two, ch. 15), he undercuts Mrs Merdle's hypocritical pretentiousness with cheerful and truthful light-hearted word-play alien to the Merdle world. When he writes that 'the street-lamps, blurred by the foggy air, burst out one after another, like so many blazing sunflowers coming into full blow all at once' (Book Two, ch. 9), the natural imagery contrasts with the gloomy, cold reality of the Strand at nightfall and makes us feel that the story is being told by an author who is freely aware of a brighter world than the London of *Little Dorrit*. Similarly, Dickens surrounds Arthur Clennam with ludicrous, absurd and cheerful language which contrasts with his depressed outlook. For example:

> There were so many lodgers in this house that the door-post seemed to be as full of bell-handles as a cathedral organ is of stops. Doubtful which might be the clarionet stop, he was considering the point, when a shuttlecock flew out of the parlour window, and alighted on his hat [Book One, ch. 9].

The author of *Little Dorrit* is a man who delights in seeing a resemblance between bell-handles and organ-stops. This playful exuberance and unconfined energy are seen most spectacularly in the language of Flora Finching, but it pervades *Little Dorrit*. From it we acquire our sense of Dickens as an author who can make us feel at the same time the suffocation of confinement in a mental prison and the exhilaration of a free mind.

Part Three: The Context

Dickens and Victorian Publishing

Public and Private Reading

We think of novel-reading as a solitary and silent activity, but the Victorians were connoisseurs of the spoken word, took pleasure in listening to sermons and speeches, and made a practice of reading novels aloud in family or other groups. Dickens read his novels aloud, both to private gatherings and to public meetings, and he was famous for his power as a reader. He greatly valued the opportunity his readings gave him for direct contact with audiences which were generally uninhibited in the expression of their feelings and responses. Hearing a novel in such an audience must have been a much more social, collaborative and dramatic experience than private reading. For the reader, the text of the novel became something like a play-script which obviously required interpretation and performance, and could be given different interpretations and performances at different times. The listener could hear the voice of the story-teller, and of the story-teller impersonating the characters, so making the role of the narrator prominent, and dialogue dramatic and theatrical, and giving a particular excitement and immediacy to the incidents of the novel. Since reading aloud is markedly slower than silent reading for most people, listeners might be less likely to miss complex poetic language or other effects which could be overlooked in rapid silent reading. Comedy would be enhanced, since laughter comes more easily to groups than to individuals. All this must have brought the experience of hearing a novel read aloud close to that of watching a play, except that with no staged action and no visible actors, the listener's visual imagination could be liberated in a way which theatrical performance might not allow.

It would be unrealistic to suggest a general revival of the Victorian practice of the public reading of novels, but it can be useful in approaching *Little Dorrit* and other novels of the period to try reading some of the text aloud, or at least to imagine how the words would sound and to ponder the effect. That may help us to understand better some important and characteristic features of Dickens's writing, such as his use of dramatic silences, or his occasional resort to authorial comments which sound like sermons or public speeches.

115

Of course the Victorians also read in solitary silence as we do, a method which has the advantage of allowing the reader to stop and reflect and to go back and re-read if necessary. Some of Dickens's effects can only be perceived by a reflective silent reader who can move backwards and forwards in the book, and only the silent reader can give adequate thought to the means by which Dickens achieves those effects. Perhaps the ideal approach would be to hear at least part of the novel read aloud, and then to embark on a private, reflective reading, much as we may read the text of a Shakespearean play after seeing a performance, each experience enhancing the other.

Reading on the Instalment Plan

Whether the first readers of *Little Dorrit* read it in silence or heard it read aloud, they experienced the novel in a way which is decidedly unfamiliar to us – by instalments. Dickens wrote the book between 1855 and 1857, and it was first published in those years as a serial, like all his novels. *Little Dorrit* was issued in twenty monthly parts, each containing three or four chapters (except that, as I have already mentioned, the last two parts, containing the last six chapters of the novel, were published together). Each part had to make some kind of narrative sense of its own, but its ending had to leave the reader looking forward to the next instalment. There was plenty of time to think about each part and to speculate about what was going to happen next, but it was correspondingly difficult to remember past instalments and the development of the story. It took the first readers of *Little Dorrit* eighteen months to reach the end of the novel, and only then would it have been possible for them to see the work as a whole. Not until the instalments were all issued did Dickens publish a single-volume edition of the novel, and he then thought it necessary to add a Preface which asks that the 'weaving' of the book should be 'looked at in its completed state' with 'the pattern finished'. The special requirements of serial publication partly explain some of the recurrent features of *Little Dorrit* which are redundant in a complete volume but useful aids to the reader's memory in a serial, such as the repeated reminders of the physical idiosyncrasies of characters whose appearances in the story may be separated by months.

Why did Dickens always choose this method of publication, which was difficult for him (each instalment had to be an exact length) as well as for his readers, when other writers of the period seldom or never did so? Serial publication allowed him to reach many readers who could not find the large sum required to buy a volume edition, but who could afford regular small payments for part-issues. In Dickens's time, novels were usually published in three volumes costing a guinea and a half, about £60 in modern values. At that price a publisher could make a satisfactory profit on an edition of only 500 copies, but the readership would be small and financially and socially exclusive. There were no free public libraries in Dickens's time, and private circulating libraries had subscriptions which put them out of reach of all but the fairly well off. In contrast, monthly instalments could be profitably sold at one shilling, about £1.90 to us, and many more people could afford to buy them. More than 30,000 copies of the first number of *Little Dorrit* were sold when it first appeared, making Dickens's readership very much larger than that of other contemporary novelists, and generally less wealthy and privileged. Some copies were bought by readers who, unable to manage even one shilling a month on their own, clubbed together in groups. And since, as we have seen, Victorian novels were often read aloud, instalments could and did reach even the illiterate.

The success of this method of publication depended upon some characteristically Victorian economic and technological developments. Paper-making, printing and binding had become much faster and cheaper, so that large numbers of copies could be rapidly prepared. These could then be sent quickly and reliably throughout the country on the newly created railways and put on sale via the network of wholesalers and retailers who distributed the products of the rapidly expanding Victorian newspaper industry. Copies could thus be sold by newsagents and stationers as well as by booksellers, which greatly increased the number of opportunities for sales.

From the publisher's point of view, instalment publication had other advantages too. Profitable advertisements could be included in the instalments and cash-flow was good, since only a small portion of the capital cost of printing the book had to be laid out at any one time. Payments came in quickly and could be used to finance the next instalment. Dickens's part-issues were a creation of this new Victorian system, and, in an important sense, representative of it. Cheap serial publication was an expression of the power of Victorian ingenuity and organization to reduce costs and widen access to literature. I suspect that every part-issue, whatever its contents, carried that implicit democratic message. At any rate, there is no doubt that serial publication was decisive in helping to make Dickens the most widely circulated and most financially successful novelist of the age.

Dickens and *Little Dorrit*

Little Dorrit in Dickens's Literary Career

We tend to think of Charles Dickens (1812–70) as a typically Victorian author, but he died halfway through the Queen's long reign, and his formative years were pre-Victorian. In many ways he was hostile to characteristic Victorian developments, and he became a radical and comprehensive critic of Victorian civilization. Before he became a professional writer Dickens worked as a lawyer's clerk and as a Parliamentary reporter, experiences which left him with an abiding contempt for the English legal system, and for Parliament and the political parties. He remained a journalist all his life, contributing to newspapers and periodicals, and from 1850 onwards editing and writing for his own journals, first *Household Words* and later *All the Year Round*.

Dickens's literary fame began in 1836–7 with the runaway success of *The Pickwick Papers*, a comic novel which contemporaries found uproariously funny. It fixed Dickens's reputation with some of his readers who wanted him to write more humorous works like *Pickwick* and complained when he didn't. As his art developed and his sales increased, Dickens found that the literary intelligentsia became more and more hostile to him. From 1846 onwards he embarked on a series of novels which are comprehensively critical of Victorian life: *Dombey and Son* (1846–8), *Bleak House* (1852–3), *Hard Times* (1854) and *Little Dorrit* (1855–7). Contemporary reviewers were often upset by Dickens's increasing social and political radicalism and dismissed him as an unscrupulous, ill-educated demagogue, too popular to be a genuine literary artist. Others disliked the increasingly sombre tone of his work. Although his sales continued to grow, reviewers often saw Dickens's literary career as a continuing decline, with *Little Dorrit* at the nadir of his achievement – a commonly held view in the nineteenth century. By contrast, in our more pessimistic age *Little Dorrit* has often been thought Dickens's greatest work.

In many ways Dickens's position in the 1850s was difficult. He was a popular entertainer with a reputation as a humorist whose books, in instalments, sold more copies than any other author's. He was also an artist who took the writing of fiction very seriously at a time when the novel was often regarded as an essentially inferior and trivial literary form, fit only for light entertainment (poetry had the prestige). In a decade of increasing prosperity and of national, commercial and industrial self-confidence he was becoming more and more hostile to Victorian institutions and behaviour. Just how badly Dickens's work accorded with the social, political and literary preferences of the influential classes, and how offensive they found it, can be seen from the contemporary reception of *Little Dorrit* (some representative reviews are collected by Philip Collins in *Dickens: The Critical Heritage*). There were bitter complaints that the Barnacles and the Circumlocution Office misrepresented English institutions and the governing classes, and might incite the lower classes to discontent with their lot. Even reviewers who shared Dickens's political opinions thought that a novel, which should provide easy, cheerful and reassuring entertainment, was not the place for them.

The same limited view of the novel's functions pervades other objections from disappointed reviewers who complained that the hero and heroine weren't as lively, good-looking and attractive as they should have been, and that well-suited couples, such as Arthur Clennam and Pet Meagles, never seemed to marry. There were objections to the unpleasant and morally dubious characters so prominent in *Little Dorrit* – for example, Mr Dorrit was thought too selfish, Mr F.'s Aunt too insane, Miss Wade too cruel and unusual to appear in a novel – and complaints that the villains did not suffer as they deserved and the good characters did not prosper as they should have done. One reviewer thought that Dickens's literary methods demanded too much attention from the reader; for example, his way of revealing Mrs General's thoughts by the movement of her gloves was no doubt true to life, but it wearied readers who were less interested than Dickens in the subtleties of human nature. Many complained that the book was far too gloomy and that the ending was neither happy nor conclusive. And of course Mrs Clennam upset those who shared her religious outlook and believed in the strict observance of Sunday.

In general, the tone of contemporary reviews of *Little Dorrit* is very hostile and dismissive, and there is no doubt that in writing as he did Dickens knowingly collided with the wishes and expectations of those of his readers who wrote reviews for literary journals. But as his sales continued and increased, he could afford to ignore his critics and write as he wished, expressing in his fiction the social and political despair and personal distress which, as we shall see, he felt in the years when *Little Dorrit* was written.

Little Dorrit and Dickens's Life

Dickens wrote *Little Dorrit*, his saddest novel, between 1855 and 1857 in what were probably the most unhappy years of his adult life. He was unusually restless, often travelling abroad and throwing himself into strenuous activities of all kinds, apparently as a distraction from his distress. All this is well described by his friend and biographer John Forster in his *Life of Charles Dickens*, which anyone interested in Dickens's life should read. The main cause seems to have been Dickens's increasing estrangement from his wife. In January 1855 Dickens wrote to Forster asking 'Why is it, that . . . a sense comes always crushing in on me now, when I fall into low spirits, as of one happiness I have missed in life, and one friend and companion I have never made?' In April 1856 Dickens writes that his life is 'laden with plot and plan and care and worry', asks whether he will ever regain his former good spirits, and adds, 'I find . . . the skeleton in my domestic closet is becoming a pretty big one.' In 1858, the year after *Little Dorrit* was finished, Dickens at last separated from his wife. Of course none of this is directly represented in the novel. But it may be that Arthur Clennam's melancholy and sense of loss reflect some of Dickens's own middle-aged depression in these years, and that the oppressive sense of confinement in *Little Dorrit* expresses some of his own desperation. However, it would be wrong to conclude that Dickens's imagination was dominated by his own painful experiences, as we can see from the use he makes in the novel of an extraordinary incident in his own life.

As a young man, Dickens had fallen passionately in love with a young lady, Maria Beadnell, the daughter of a banker. Her parents did not regard Dickens, at the time a novice newspaper reporter with an insolvent father, as an eligible suitor, and, whether for that reason or another, Maria Beadnell did not return his love. He was deeply hurt, so much so that he was unable to write about the episode in a fragment of auto-biography he wrote for Forster some fifteen years later. Unexpectedly, early in 1855, just as he was beginning to think about *Little Dorrit* and had written to Forster about his sense that someone was missing from his life, he received a letter from Maria, who, like Dickens, was by now middle-aged and married. Dickens replied in a series of letters which revealed the most intense romantic memories and expectations, and arranged a meeting which was a sad and ludicrous disappointment. Maria was now fat, talkative, very middle-aged and too fond of brandy, nothing like the youthful romantic sweetheart he had optimistically expected to find again after a quarter of a century. The episode is comically echoed in Arthur Clennam's relations with Flora Finching. The novelist who could create Flora out of such a disappointing and embarrassing experience was obviously capable of distancing himself from his feelings and transmuting them into a work of art, and was clearly not permanently sunk in gloom.

I draw much the same conclusion from Dickens's treatment in *Little Dorrit* of a subject which must have revived memories of the most painful experience of his early life. His father, John Dickens, was a cheerful and hard-working civil servant who enjoyed spending money and unfortunately spent more than he earned. So, after a happy and imaginative childhood (nothing like Arthur Clennam's), Dickens found his adolescence blighted by financial troubles. First, he was taken away from school and sent to work in a small factory, labelling bottles. Then, at the age of fourteen, he was left in a lodging house while the rest of the family went to live in the Marshalsea with his father, who had been arrested for debt. Dickens used to visit the prison on Sundays and came to know it and its inhabitants well, although he never spent a night behind bars.

He recalled the miseries of this time in the autobiographical fragment already mentioned, which was published after his death in Book One of Forster's *Life of Charles Dickens*. In it he describes his younger self as he 'lounged about the streets, insufficiently and unsatisfactorily fed', with 'no advice, no counsel, no encouragement, no consolation, no support, from anyone', and in peril of becoming 'a little robber or a little vagabond'. No doubt these experiences gave the adult novelist strong personal reasons for his interest in the Marshalsea prison, and in the fate of child-victims and the outcast poor. But it would be wrong to think that *Little Dorrit* simply recounts his own life as described in his memoir. There is no character in the novel who represents the young Dickens's experiences of the Marshalsea, and no sign that he was absorbed in his past sufferings and compelled to relieve them by writing autobiographical novels about his past unhappiness.

Dickens and the Historical Context

Dickens's Social and Political Despair

During the years in which *Little Dorrit* was planned and written (1855–7), Dickens's view of the social and political condition of England was darker than it had ever been before, or was to be later. On occasion he fell into despair. We find him writing to John Forster on 3 February 1855, 'I don't see a gleam of hope,' and to another old friend, Macready the actor, on 4 October 1855, 'I have no present political faith or hope – not a grain.' Characteristically, Dickens's despair found active and energetic expression. He wrote a series of articles in *Household Words* attacking what he thought was amiss, relieved his feelings in *Little Dorrit* (he told Macready that Book One, chapter 10, let off 'indignant steam which would otherwise blow me up'), and, for the first and last time in his life, joined an avowedly political organization, the Administrative Reform Association, which in 1855 tried (and failed) to reform civil and military administration.

What were the causes of Dickens's indignation and despair and what relation has the world of *Little Dorrit* to the England of 1855? Dickens gave part of his own answer in the Preface to *Little Dorrit*, in which he briefly justifies his fiction of the Barnacles and the Circumlocution Office as essentially true to life, referring to the Crimean War and other contemporary events, as well as to 'the common experience of an Englishman'. The common experience of an Englishman of Dickens's time is not of course something we can hope to recover, but some knowledge of the historical context to which Dickens refers can help us to understand *Little Dorrit* better, because it is a remarkably topical book and deeply responsive to the age in which it was written, as its author and its first readers recognized. Of course history is controversial, and there is no agreed version of the 1850s which can simply be invoked to resolve literary disputes. Nevertheless, there is good evidence to suggest that Dickens's fictional portrait of an England governed by self-seeking and incompetent aristocratic politicians and obstructive bureaucrats, swindled by crooked financiers and tormented by gloomy and restrictive religion is substantially accurate, as he claimed. Some of this evidence comes, ironically, from reports presented to that Parliament which

Dickens despised. It would be wrong to expect scrupulous fairness from Dickens who, like other satirists, does not attempt to tell the whole truth, but his fictional world, in my opinion, is solidly based on fact. As Ruskin wrote in *Unto This Last*, 'allowing for his manner of telling them, the things he tells us are always true'.

The Civil Service and the Circumlocution Office

Is the Circumlocution Office at least in part a recognizable portrait of the government and Civil Service in 1855? The main authority on the Civil Service at the time was the *Report on the Organization of the Permanent Civil Service* (1854), written for Parliament by Stafford Northcote, M.P., and Sir Charles Trevelyan, an eminent official. The Report found that the organization of the Civil Service was 'far from perfect'; that posts in government employment were chiefly sought by the 'unambitious' and the 'indolent or incapable' who could not succeed in competitive professions, but could obtain 'an honourable livelihood with little labour' in the Civil Service; that posts were obtained by family and political influence; that men of 'very slender ability and perhaps of questionable character' were given important positions because of 'family or political interest'; that entrants to the Service were not trained; that civil servants spent most of their time on routine duties such as the copying of papers; that promotion was by seniority, irrespective of merit; and that the poor quality of civil servants led to public 'complaints of official delays, official evasions of difficulty, and official indisposition to improvement'. To reform these abuses, Northcote and Trevelyan proposed a system of compulsory examinations for candidates for the Service, and promotion by merit alone, practices which became the foundation of the modern Civil Service when, despite determined resistance, they were at last fully introduced in 1870, the year of Dickens's death.

In general, then, the Civil Service as described by the *Report* does resemble the Circumlocution Office. Rank, relationship and political influence are preferred to merit, the sham replaces the real and the nation suffers, both in fact as seen by Northcote and Trevelyan, and in fiction as created by Dickens. The main difference is that Dickens writes satirically as though the Circumlocution Office deliberately intended to produce general stagnation and futility – 'How not to do it'. Northcote and Trevelyan see administrative inefficiency as an unfortunate and unintended consequence of the use of the Civil Service by the privileged classes as a means of helping friends, relations and political allies, and as a source of employment for the otherwise unemployable. But as that had been going on for years, why was Dickens so angry about it in 1855? The immediate cause of his indignation was the appalling mismanagement of the Crimean War during the winter of 1854–5, when military disasters abroad revealed what was amiss at home.

A Russian War: 'How not to do it' in the Crimea

In the winter of 1854–5, eight regiments of the British expeditionary force in the Crimea lost three quarters of their men to causes other than enemy action. This disaster was reported in detail as it happened by war correspondents, of whom the most famous and best informed was the correspondent of *The Times*, William Howard Russell. At first his reports were not believed, but in the end not even government spokesmen could deny their truth. The result was unprecedented public indignation, a series of Parliamentary inquiries, the findings of the first of which were published as the *Reports from the Select Committee on the Army before Sebastopol* (1855), and some belated action which saved the remnant of the army. Dickens read Russell's reports, summarized them and the Parliamentary inquiries in *Household Words* and published articles by serving soldiers. What was it about this 'Russian War' which in Dickens's view justified his portrayal of the Barnacles and the Circumlocution Office?

In the British army of the period there was no relation between rank and merit. Commissions were bought, so that only wealthy men could achieve high rank and capable soldiers who lacked money could not obtain promotion. Officers considered it ungentlemanly to study their profession seriously, and nearly all of them (even staff officers) were untrained. Most of the officers in the Crimea were also inexperienced, since there had been no wars in Europe since 1815. The British army in India had of course been involved in continuous warfare, and its soldiers were highly skilled, but they were regarded as socially inferior. So, when the cavalry generals were chosen for the Crimea, men of experience and known ability were passed over in favour of well-connected, aristocratic novices of limited intelligence such as Lord Lucan and Lord Cardigan, who between them managed to blunder away many of their troops in the famous charge of the Light Brigade at Balaclava. The same lack of professionalism was found among junior officers, many of whom gave up their commissions in the middle of the campaign. More than two hundred resigned in two days in December 1854, leaving some regiments nearly without officers (we recall that Edmund Sparkler had left the army because he didn't like it).

Not only did promotion go to the Barnacles, but the equipment of the army showed a Circumlocutionary preference for appearance over reality. The life of a cavalryman depended on the sharpness of his sword and the speed of his horse. If a novelist depicted an army which deliberately kept its swords blunt and its equipment as cumbrous as possible, he would be accused of 'symbolism' or 'absurd exaggeration', depending on the standpoint of the critic. It is hard to believe, but it is nonetheless entirely true, that the British cavalry in the 1850s was equipped with blunt swords. The reason was that in the performance of manoeuvres on the barrack-square, there was a great deal of ritualized drawing and sheathing of swords, which made a much more satisfying noise if the scabbards were metal. It also blunted the swords. Two days after being sharpened, a sword was blunt and innocuous. Wooden or leather scabbards which would have preserved the edge of the blade were rejected as unspectacular. So it was that at Balaclava the Heavy Brigade found itself outnumbered six to one, with swords so blunt that they could only be used like sticks.

Not only were the cavalry's weapons inoffensive, their accoutrements were absurdly heavy. A fully dressed trooper weighed about twenty-two stone and was encumbered by stiff and tight clothing. He was also brightly coloured and highly conspicuous. This made him a splendid show on the parade ground, and an easy victim for the lightly armed Cossack horsemen in the Crimea. The cavalry was of course the stronghold of fashionable incompetence, but even the infantry suffered. Their uniform included the 'stock', the stiff high collar which obstructed the blood supply to the head and made it impossible to turn the head without turning the body. Russell described a short march of six miles before the fighting began during which seventy men out of ninety fainted because of their stocks and tight coats.

Such a preference for appearance over reality in the equipment of an army suggests either an unconscious pacifism or determined stupidity. When it is self-destructive, we may well think that 'How not to do it' was the motto of the army command as well as of the Circumlocution Office.

The aim of the Crimean War was to hurt Russia and relieve her pressure on Turkey. However, by the time the British army arrived the Turks had already beaten off a Russian invasion, leaving no very obvious task for the British expeditionary force. In these circumstances the Cabi-

net decided to invade and assault Sebastopol, although there was no
reliable intelligence of the strength of the Russian defensive forces. The
army found itself trying to besiege a fortress defended by a larger gar-
rison. No advance was possible, and any attempt at retreat would have
invited annihilation. The army had to stand its ground, wait for supplies
and reinforcements, and discourage Russian attacks by acts of military
impudence. This was the hazardous position into which the imprudence
of statesmen had flung the army. What turned danger into disaster was
the efforts of the Commissariat.

The Commissariat, the army's main supply department, was a civilian
organization under the direct control of the Treasury, headed by Sir
Charles Trevelyan of the Northcote–Trevelyan Report. There were other
supply organizations too: the military Quartermaster-General's Department was responsible for the supply of ammunition and the repair
of the roads, and the civilian Purveyor's Department provided, or was
supposed to provide, medical supplies and invalid diets. It was all very
complex, and the soldiers frequently had great difficulty in finding out
who was supposed to be supplying what, but there can be no doubt that
the civilian Commissariat was responsible for the supply of food, clothing
and shelter for men and horses.

The mortality in the winter of 1854 was due, in the words of the
Parliamentary Commissioners, to 'overwork, exposure to wet and cold,
improper food, insufficient clothing during part of the winter, and insufficient shelter from inclement weather'. The overwork was the responsibility of the Commander-in-Chief, and was an inevitable result of
the dangerous position of the army, but all the rest was the fault of the
Commissariat. This department had steamships to transport food, and
ready access to the markets of Constantinople. There was no shortage of
supplies or transport, and no lack of money to pay for them. Yet
nevertheless a British force was left less than seven miles from a safe
harbour, without food, clothes or shelter, its troops dying at the rate of a
hundred a day.

These were the dire consequences of administrative ineptitude. The
personnel of the Commissariat were mostly Treasury clerks who brought
their Treasury ways to a situation in which maladministration could,
and did, cause the unnecessary deaths of thousands. What the soldiers
most needed was an adequate supply of fresh food – meat, vegetables
and bread. All these were readily and cheaply available near the Crimea.
Unfortunately, the regulations of the Commissariat were based on the
assumption that an army on campaign would forage for itself, providing

its own fresh food and fuel to cook it with. Consequently all the Commissariat would supply was the regulation preserved food (chiefly salt meat) brought at great expense all the way from England. There was no fresh food or fuel to be found in the Crimean winter and so the army went without, with the predictable result of frightful mortality from disease. It even happened that at the time when the army was suffering badly from scurvy, stores of lime-juice and rice, ordered not as food but as medical provisions, arrived at the harbour but were not issued. The Commissariat was not obliged to inform the Commander of what was in store, but only of what had already been issued to the troops – and the lime-juice had not been given out because no one told the army that it was available.

This would perhaps be dismissed as incredible in fiction. But it happened more than once. In December 1854 and January 1855, 12,000 great-coats were in store at Balaclava, but they were not issued because the regulations forbade the issue of more than one great-coat per man every three years. It was of no relevance that the soldiers had worn out their great-coats on active service and were dying from exposure – they would have to wait another two years, just as though they were in Aldershot. Similarly, stores of trousers and rugs were not issued, and requests for fuel were met with the reminder that it was the custom of the service to forage for firewood. It didn't matter that there were no trees left round Sebastopol. The army could, and did, go cold.

The worst disasters followed the breakdown of the road between Balaclava harbour and the camp round Sebastopol. The road was destroyed by the passage of the artillery and the Quartermaster-General was unable to repair it as he had no soldiers to spare and no trained artificers. The Commissariat's baggage animals were in any case far too few and soon broke down under the strain. The troops then had to carry their supplies themselves, if they could.

These larger administrative deficiencies were reinforced by petty obstructiveness. Officials would insist on precise compliance with unnecessarily complicated formalities. The soldiers did not attempt to take the horses to Balaclava to feed because the required formalities were so obstructive. On at least one occasion food for the troops was refused because the requisition form was signed half an inch too low. Urgently needed stores arriving by sea at Balaclava harbour were turned away if not accompanied by the proper forms. A cargo of cabbages was actually thrown into the water on the grounds that it was not specifically consigned to anyone in particular. Contemporary readers of *Little Dorrit* who heard in Book Two, chapter 2, that Mrs General's former husband had been 'a stiff commissariat officer of sixty, famous as a martinet', will have remembered the Commissariat's insistence on the proprieties in the Crimea, and that memory must have given a grim tone to Mrs General which the modern reader may miss.

A soldier in the Crimea was much safer under Russian attack in the trenches round Sebastopol than he was when being cared for by the British Army's Medical Corps. There was no proper transport for the sick, as the ambulance corps had been staffed by old-age pensioners who had broken down. There was no medicine in the hospital at Balaclava. If a sick or wounded soldier survived the sea voyage to Scutari, he found himself in a desperately overcrowded hospital, built over a sewer, without adequate nursing, diet, medicines or clothing. Many died. In February 1855 42 per cent of the patients perished.

An abundance of supplies had been sent from England, but most of it had disappeared somewhere in transit. Very little arrived at Scutari, and it was nobody's responsibility to make sure that it did. If the Hospital Superintendent wanted stores, he would formally requisition the Purveyor for them. The Purveyor would then requisition the Commissariat, who would usually reply, 'None in store.' The Purveyor would then report this to the Hospital Superintendent, who would do no more about it. All had done their duty. It was nobody's business to set about getting the supplies, for the want of which men were dying. Provided the paperwork had been properly done, the requirements of the system were satisfied.

Those responsible for this disaster were rewarded and promoted. The Superintendent of the hospital, who had reported, 'Nothing is lacking,' at a time when there were no supplies, was awarded a K.C.B. – 'Knight of the Crimean Burial grounds', as Florence Nightingale bitterly commented. Those who attempted to improve the situation – chiefly Florence Nightingale – met determined and unscrupulous opposition from officials and politicians. But, with public support, they were at last able to apply well-known principles of health and hygiene to the hospital. A Sanitary Commission removed 556 handcarts of 'rubbish' and 24 dead animals from the hospital, and the death rate fell to 2 per cent in June 1855. However, it was to take Florence Nightingale and her supporters several years to overcome official and political opposition to the reform and improvement of all army medical services.

These British calamities contrasted sharply with the successes of the much larger French army in the Crimea. Throughout the winter of

1854–5, the French troops were adequately provided with food, clothing, shelter, fuel, transport and medical supplies. As their positions adjoined the British their superiority was well known, particularly as they were so well supplied that they were even able to help the British army with transport. They had given a demonstration of 'How to do it' in conditions identical to the British army's, and so removed any vestige of excuse for the British disasters. Their advantage was that their supply department was not staffed by British civil servants and their strategy and organization were not directed by a British Cabinet which behaved as though it were trying to destroy its own troops.

A Court of Inquiry at Chelsea

Lord Aberdeen's administration fell in January 1855 following the revelations of the winter disasters in the Crimea, Lord Aberdeen still heroically claiming that the reports were 'grossly exaggerated'. It was replaced by the Cabinet of Lord Palmerston, which was expected to make reforms, and which, under Parliamentary pressure, appointed two Commissioners, Sir John McNeill and Colonel Tulloch, to inquire into the supplies of the army in the Crimea. The *Report of the Commission of Inquiry into the Supplies of the British Army in the Crimea* (1856), made it clear, with abundant evidence, that the destruction of the army had been unnecessary and mostly the consequence of a faulty system of supplies – a compound of inefficiency, stupidity, indifference and destructive bureaucratic routine.

The *Report* was judicious and restrained in tone, and though clearly indicating what had gone wrong and why, mostly avoided attributing particular blame. It was perhaps all the more embarrassing for that, as the entire system was indicted, and this may explain why Lord Palmerston did not take the obvious course of blaming everything on his predecessors. The whole system of government had been called into question, not merely the acts of a particular Cabinet, and that system remained essentially unchanged. Rather than attempt reform, the government decided to throw discredit on the *Report*.

It was impossible to prevent publication of the *Report* in January 1856, but the government made its attitude clear by promoting and decorating most of those in positions of authority in the Crimea and refusing any reward to McNeill and Tulloch. It also appointed a Board of General Officers to assemble at the Royal Hospital, Chelsea, 'to inquire into the statements contained in the reports of Sir John McNeill and Col. Tulloch, and the evidence taken by them relative thereto, animadverting upon the conduct of certain officers on the General Staff . . .'. This was the Court of Inquiry at Chelsea, referred to by Dickens in his 1857 Preface to *Little Dorrit* as a justification for his portrayal of the Circumlocution Office. (The notes to the Penguin edition of the novel, p. 900, confuse this Inquiry with the earlier *Reports from the Select Committee on the Army before Sebastopol* of 1855, chaired by J. A. Roebuck.)

The Board was composed of seven generals, none of whom had been in the Crimea and all of whom belonged to the same political party (Lord Palmerston's). Their terms of reference were unusual: they were to inquire into the correctness of the conclusions of a previous Commission, without recourse to the evidence on which that Commission had based its findings. In the end the Board exonerated all the officers who complained to it from any charge of mismanagement or neglect in the Crimea.

Lord Lucan, the commander of the cavalry, was cleared of any responsibility for the loss of the horses which died from exposure. The Board agreed with his plea that he had done nothing to shelter the horses because nothing could have been done, ignoring evidence that the materials for temporary and effective shelters had been readily available, and indeed successfully used in one regiment. Lord Cardigan, the commander of the light cavalry, was cleared of any blame for refusing to allow his horses to fetch provender from Balaclava when the Commissariat transport system had broken down and the horses were starving to death. The Board accepted Cardigan's assertion that his orders required him to keep all his horses in the line, so that none could be spared to fetch provender, ignoring the obvious point that horses visibly dying of starvation were no use in the line, and it was fatuous to allege military necessity as a reason for not feeding them.

General Airey, the Quartermaster-General, who was responsible for some of the army's supplies at a time when soldiers were dying of exposure, was also exonerated. The Board accepted his argument that his department had no means of receiving, keeping or transporting stores, ignoring evidence that he had organized the supply of an immense weight of ordnance stores, especially ammunition, to an army clothed in rags and dying of exposure for lack of the warm clothing and tents which abounded in the stores at Balaclava. Mr Filder, the civilian who, under Sir Charles Trevelyan of the Treasury, was in charge of the Commissariat, was cleared of any blame for the deficiencies in the army's supplies. The Board laid the blame on the Treasury, which had failed to respond promptly or fully enough to Filder's repeated requests for supplies of pressed hay from England to feed the transport animals, with the result that the transport system had broken down and the Commissariat had been unable to transfer enough supplies from the stores to the soldiers.

This comfortable conclusion ignored the obvious point that there was no need to depend on supplies of pressed hay brought all the way from England when there was plenty of cheap fodder to be bought locally – Constantinople was the emporium of the East – and plenty of ships to bring it in. The experience of the winter of 1855–6, when the army, now three times the size of the previous winter, with the same resources in reach, was adequately supplied with fresh food for men and fodder for animals from Constantinople, had shown beyond doubt that the sufferings of 1854–5 were unnecessary. But the Board chose to ignore that.

As a result of these illogical and disreputable official attempts to exonerate some of those whose stupidity and blind adherence to routine had caused the most appalling and unnecessary suffering and death, the Chelsea Board became popularly known as 'the White-washing Board'. Newspaper comments on these Circumlocutionary attempts to brazen out the Crimean disasters were overwhelmingly unfavourable, and certainly not confined to those who shared Dickens's political attitudes. The *Saturday Review*, a weekly paper very hostile to Dickens, wrote on 26 July 1856:

> We had heard that about one third of the force despatched to the East in the autumn of 1854 had been suffered to perish from cold, starvation and fatigue. In our unmilitary ignorance, we fancied that this frightful destruction of life was wrong, and that it could only have arisen from grievous neglect or incapacity in some quarter or other . . . The short result of the long inquiry is, that two prompt and ingenious cavalry officers contrived to destroy their horses and dismount their force – that the most efficient of Quartermaster-Generals, seconded by a faultless staff of subordinates, left the army to die of cold – and that a Commissary-General of inventive resources and comprehensive views could neither feed the soldiers nor subsist his beasts of burden.

Mr Merdle's Wonderful Bank

In his Preface to *Little Dorrit*, Dickens defends what he ironically calls 'that extravagant conception, Mr Merdle', by referring to various topical or recent financial scandals, of which he gives few details, assuming that they are already known to his readers. These scandals greatly resemble Mr Merdle's career, revealing widespread greed and worship of money, and the encouragement of fraudulent financiers by people who should have known better. Dickens refers first to 'the Rail-road share epoch', the period of intense speculation in railway shares in the 1840s, during which George Hudson, the 'Railway King' rose to a position of wealth, power and fame. Hudson controlled the Midland and North-Eastern railway systems, became an M.P., gave spectacular parties for the rich and powerful in his London home and was widely respected and admired as a financial genius. The sudden collapse of his financial empire with a loss of some £80,000,000 to investors revealed that he had been guilty of systematic fraud.

Dickens also mentions 'a certain Irish bank' and 'one or two other equally laudable enterprises'. The Irish bank was the Tipperary Bank, which failed in February 1856. The collapse revealed that one of the directors, John Sadleir, an M.P. and a Junior Lord of the Treasury in 1853, had been engaged in widespread fraud. Sadleir committed suicide by drinking poison from a silver jug on Hampstead Heath on 16 February 1856. Shortly afterwards Dickens wrote to Forster, 'I had the general idea of the Society business before the Sadleir affair, but I shaped Mr Merdle himself out of that precious rascality,' and 'Mr Merdle's complaint, which you will find in the end to be fraud and forgery, came into my mind as the last drop in the silver cream-jug on Hampstead-heath.'

The Royal British Bank, mentioned by Dickens as an example of how 'a bad design will sometimes claim to be a good and an expressly religious design', failed on 3 September 1856, creating 'a world of misery and ruin' for its depositors. Many of them were relatively poor people whom the bank had deliberately attracted by offering its services in districts of London not usually served by financial institutions. The directors had claimed this a virtue while swindling their clients. Passing judgment on the directors, Mr Commissioner Holroyd said in the Court of Bankruptcy: 'I do not believe that a scene of greater recklessness, fraud and criminality of conduct in the management of a banking establishment was ever exhibited in a court of justice.' (See *The Times*, 4 September and 8 October 1856, and 15 May 1857.) These financial abuses are the immediate historical context of Mr Merdle's 'wonderful bank' in *Little Dorrit*.

Barnacles and Benefactors

In a witty and cogent *Household Words* article (1 August 1857) replying to criticism of *Little Dorrit*, Dickens cited the career of Rowland Hill, the postal reformer, as an example of how Circumlocutionary governments obstructed inventors like Daniel Doyce who had projects for the public benefit. Hill was a versatile and creative engineer. As a railway director he pioneered express trains and Sunday excursion trains. Among his inventions was a cheap and efficient rotary press for newspapers which the Treasury refused to allow to be used because it wanted to continue the old system of taxing newspapers by impressing a stamp on each copy at the Stamp Office.

Undeterred by this contact with the official mind, Hill began to study the Post Office, which was so expensive that most of the population could not afford to send letters, and came to the unexpected conclusion that if postage rates were not related to distance they could be much cheaper. Hill submitted a scheme on these lines to the Prime Minister, Lord Melbourne, in 1837, but was ignored. Then he published a pamphlet which attracted public support despite being ridiculed by officials, especially those in the Post Office who stood to lose customary fees if the scheme were introduced. Public pressure led to the appointment of a Parliamentary committee which recommended in 1838 that Hill's proposals should be tried. The government at first refused and then gave way in 1839 after more public pressure. Hill was given a two-year temporary appointment with no direct authority over the Post Office officials, who systematically obstructed him. In 1842 he was dismissed by Peel, who was now Prime Minister. In the following year Hill petitioned Parliament for an inquiry into the Post Office, but nothing was done. In 1846 a public subscription raised £16,000 as a testimonial to Hill (about £600,000 in modern values), and the year after the Prime Minister of the day, Lord John Russell, offered him another subordinate position in the Post Office. For eight years this arrangement continued, with Hill again impeded by officials, until in 1854, just before *Little Dorrit* was written, he was given sole power over the Post Office.

Hill's transformation of the Post Office was a great benefit to his fellow-citizens, particularly to the poorer classes, who for the first time could afford to send letters. The only losers were officials and place-holders who had benefited from the old system of fees and patronage. And yet these men, supported by their political friends, were able to obstruct the improvements for years, first by an open refusal to consider the reforms, and then by appearing to comply, but in reality impeding Hill as much as possible and trying to wear him down. In his article Dickens comments on Hill's career that 'the Circumlocution Office most characteristically opposed him as long as opposition was in any way possible'. A fuller account of Hill's difficulties can be found in the *Dictionary of National Biography*. The Barnacles' fictional treatment of Daniel Doyce was solidly based on fact.

Sabbatarians

Sunday Observance was particularly topical when Book One, chapter 3, of *Little Dorrit* was published in December 1855. Sabbatarians believed that the rules prescribed in the Old Testament for the observance of the Jewish Sabbath should also apply to the Christian Sunday, and in particular that work should be prohibited on a Sunday. By the mid-nineteenth century, laws had been passed which produced the English Sunday evoked in chapter 3, when everything was 'bolted and barred that could by possibility furnish relief to an overworked people'. (Places of public amusement were closed because some people would have had to work to keep them open.)

There was an attempt at further legislation in the summer of 1855, when Lord Robert Grosvenor, M.P. for Middlesex (the 'county member' contemptuously referred to in chapter 3), introduced a Private Member's Bill, with government support, to put down Sunday trading in London. This would have prevented people buying fresh food on Sundays. The wealthier classes would have been unaffected, since they had cool larders in which to keep their food. But the poor, living in overcrowded and unhygienic conditions, had nowhere to store food safely and had to buy it daily. As Dickens notes in chapter 3, 'people lived so unwholesomely, that fair water put into their crowded rooms on Saturday night would be corrupt on Sunday morning', so how could they possibly store food for Sunday? The Bill was strongly opposed outside Parliament, and there were violent demonstrations in and around Hyde Park on 24 June, which resumed on successive Sundays for several weeks, even though Lord Robert deferred to popular pressure and withdrew his Bill on 2 July.

Dickens had always been opposed to Sabbatarianism, which he regarded as a cruel perversion of Christianity, and he published articles and a pamphlet which spoke up for the right of the poor to enjoy themselves on Sunday. In one sense chapter 3 is a contribution to

Dickens's campaign against Sabbatarianism, and it was welcomed (or deplored) by contemporaries as an attack on the alliance of religious fanatics and politicians which had turned the poorer classes' only day of leisure into a day of gloomy monotony, and had even tried to deprive them of fresh food on Sundays. Reports of the events of 1855 can be found in *The Times* (4 May, 25 June, 2 July, 3 July) and the *Annual Register*, pp. 106–9.

Suggestions for Further Reading

The place of publication is London, unless otherwise stated

Editions

Harvey Peter Sucksmith has prepared the standard scholarly edition in the Clarendon series (Oxford, 1979).

Biography and Scholarship

John Forster's *Life of Charles Dickens* is edited by A. J. Hoppé (revised 1969). Edgar Johnson's modern biography *Charles Dickens: His Tragedy and Triumph* (revised 1977) supplements Forster. Dickens's working methods are illuminated in *Dickens at Work* (1957) by John Butt and Kathleen Tillotson, and in H. P. Sucksmith's introduction to the Clarendon edition, already mentioned.

The Historical Context

Henry Mayhew's *London Labour and the London Poor* (1851–2) gives examples of children who, like Amy Dorrit, are forced to assume the responsibilities of adults. Some of these are included in the Penguin volume of selections from Mayhew's work (published under the same title as the original, Harmondsworth, 1985); see in particular 'Of Two Orphan Flower Girls' and 'Watercress Girl' (pp. 61–8). Cecil Woodham-Smith's *Florence Nightingale: 1820–1910* (1950) contains a lively account of the Crimean disasters.

Criticism

Alan Shelston has edited a useful collection of criticism in his *Charles Dickens: Dombey and Son and Little Dorrit: A Casebook* (1985). Other helpful collections are Philip Collins's *Dickens: The Critical Heritage* (1971) and Stephen Wall's *Charles Dickens* (Harmondsworth, 1970). Many twentieth-century writers refer to *Little Dorrit*, and a selection of titles follows:

George Gissing, *Charles Dickens: A Critical Study* (1902)

G. K. Chesterton, Introduction to *Little Dorrit* (Everyman edition, 1908, often reprinted)

T. A. Jackson, *Charles Dickens: The Progress of a Radical* (1937)

Edmund Wilson, *The Wound and the Bow* (Cambridge, Mass., 1941; London, 1952)

Lionel Trilling, Introduction to *Little Dorrit* (OUP edition, Oxford, 1953)

Monroe Engel, *The Maturity of Dickens* (1959)

John Holloway, Introduction to *Little Dorrit* (Penguin edition, Harmondsworth, 1967)

J. C. Reid, *Charles Dickens's 'Little Dorrit'* (1967)

F. R. and Q. D. Leavis, *Dickens the Novelist* (1970)

John Lucas, *The Melancholy Man: A Study of Dickens's Novels* (1970, revised 1980)

Angus Wilson, *The World of Charles Dickens* (1970)

William Myers, in J. Lucas (ed.), *Literature and Politics in the Nineteenth Century* (1971)

Alexander Welsh, *The City of Dickens* (Oxford, 1971)

John Carey, *The Violent Effigy: A Study of Dickens's Imagination* (1973)

Geoffrey Thurley, *The Dickens Myth: Its Genesis and Structure* (1976)

P. J. M. Scott, *Reality and Comic Confidence in Charles Dickens* (1979)

F. S. Schwarzbach, *Dickens and the City* (1979)

Susan R. Horton, *The Reader in the Dickens World* (1981)

Dennis Walder, *Dickens and Religion* (1981)

James M. Brown, *Dickens: Novelist in the Market Place* (1982)

MORE ABOUT PENGUINS, PELICANS, PEREGRINES AND PUFFINS

ENGLISH AND AMERICAN
LITERATURE IN PENGUINS

☐ *Emma* **Jane Austen** £1.25

'I am going to take a heroine whom no one but myself will much like,'
declared Jane Austen of Emma, her most spirited and controversial
heroine in a comedy of self-deceit and self-discovery.

☐ *Tender is the Night* **F. Scott Fitzgerald** £2.95

Fitzgerald worked on seventeen different versions of this novel, and
its obsessions – idealism, beauty, dissipation, alcohol and insanity –
were those that consumed his own marriage and his life.

☐ *The Life of Johnson* **James Boswell** £2.95

Full of gusto, imagination, conversation and wit, Boswell's immortal
portrait of Johnson is as near a novel as a true biography can be, and
still regarded by many as the finest 'life' ever written. This shortened
version is based on the 1799 edition.

☐ *A House and its Head* **Ivy Compton-Burnett** £4.95

In a novel 'as trim and tidy as a hand-grenade' (as Pamela Hansford
Johnson put it), Ivy Compton-Burnett penetrates the facade of a
conventional, upper-class Victorian family to uncover a chasm of
violent emotions – jealousy, pain, frustration and sexual passion.

☐ *The Trumpet Major* **Thomas Hardy** £1.50

Although a vein of unhappy unrequited love runs through this novel,
Hardy also draws on his warmest sense of humour to portray
Wessex village life at the time of the Napoleonic wars.

☐ *The Complete Poems of Hugh MacDiarmid*

☐ Volume One £8.95
☐ Volume Two £8.95

The definitive edition of work by the greatest Scottish poet since
Robert Burns, edited by his son Michael Grieve, and W. R. Aitken.

ENGLISH AND AMERICAN LITERATURE IN PENGUINS

☐ **Main Street** **Sinclair Lewis** £4.95

The novel that added an immortal chapter to the literature of America's Mid-West, *Main Street* contains the comic essence of Main Streets everywhere.

☐ **The Compleat Angler** **Izaak Walton** £2.50

A celebration of the countryside, and the superiority of those in 1653, as now, who love *quietnesse, vertue* and, above all, *Angling*. 'No fish, however coarse, could wish for a doughtier champion than Izaak Walton' – Lord Home

☐ **The Portrait of a Lady** **Henry James** £2.50

'One of the two most brilliant novels in the language', according to F. R. Leavis, James's masterpiece tells the story of a young American heiress, prey to fortune-hunters but not without a will of her own.

☐ **Hangover Square** **Patrick Hamilton** £3.95

Part love story, part thriller, and set in the publands of London's Earls Court, this novel caught the conversational tone of a whole generation in the uneasy months before the Second World War.

☐ **The Rainbow** **D. H. Lawrence** £2.50

Written between *Sons and Lovers* and *Women in Love*, *The Rainbow* covers three generations of Brangwens, a yeoman family living on the borders of Nottinghamshire.

☐ **Vindication of the Rights of Woman**
Mary Wollstonecraft £2.95

Although Walpole once called her 'a hyena in petticoats', Mary Wollstonecraft's vision was such that modern feminists continue to go back and debate the arguments so powerfully set down here.

CLASSICS IN TRANSLATION
IN PENGUINS

☐ *Remembrance of Things Past* **Marcel Proust**

☐ Volume One: *Swann's Way, Within a Budding Grove*   £7.95
☐ Volume Two: *The Guermantes Way, Cities of the Plain*   £7.95
☐ Volume Three: *The Captive, The Fugitive, Time Regained*   £7.95

Terence Kilmartin's acclaimed revised version of C. K. Scott Moncrieff's original translation, published in paperback for the first time.

☐ *The Canterbury Tales* **Geoffrey Chaucer**   £2.95

'Every age is a Canterbury Pilgrimage . . . nor can a child be born who is not one of these characters of Chaucer' – William Blake

☐ *Gargantua & Pantagruel* **Rabelais**   £3.95

The fantastic adventures of two giants through which Rabelais (1495–1553) caricatured his life and times in a masterpiece of exuberance and glorious exaggeration.

☐ *The Brothers Karamazov* **Fyodor Dostoevsky**   £4.95

A detective story on many levels, profoundly involving the question of the existence of God, Dostoevsky's great drama of parricide and fraternal jealousy triumphantly fulfilled his aim: 'to find the man in man . . . [to] depict all the depths of the human soul.'

☐ *Fables of Aesop*   £1.95

This translation recovers all the old magic of fables in which, too often, the fox steps forward as the cynical hero and a lamb is an ass to lie down with a lion.

☐ *The Three Theban Plays* **Sophocles**   £2.95

A new translation, by Robert Fagles, of *Antigone, Oedipus the King* and *Oedipus at Colonus*, plays all based on the legend of the royal house of Thebes.

CLASSICS IN TRANSLATION
IN PENGUINS

☐ *The Treasure of the City of Ladies*
Christine de Pisan   £2.95

This practical survival handbook for women (whether royal courtiers or prostitutes) paints a vivid picture of their lives and preoccupations in France, *c.* 1405. First English translation.

☐ *La Regenta* **Leopoldo Alas**   £10.95

This first English translation of this Spanish masterpiece has been acclaimed as 'a major literary event' – *Observer*. 'Among the select band of "world novels" . . . outstandingly well translated' – John Bayley in the *Listener*

☐ *Metamorphoses* **Ovid**   £2.95

The whole of Western literature has found inspiration in Ovid's poem, a golden treasury of myths and legends that are linked by the theme of transformation.

☐ *Darkness at Noon* **Arthur Koestler**   £2.50

'Koestler approaches the problem of ends and means, of love and truth and social organization, through the thoughts of an Old Bolshevik, Rubashov, as he awaits death in a G.P.U. prison' – *New Statesman*

☐ *War and Peace* **Leo Tolstoy**   £4.95

'A complete picture of human life;' wrote one critic, 'a complete picture of the Russia of that day; a complete picture of everything in which people place their happiness and greatness, their grief and humiliation.'

☐ *The Divine Comedy: 1 Hell* **Dante**   £2.25

A new translation by Mark Musa, in which the poet is conducted by the spirit of Virgil down through the twenty-four closely described circles of hell.

Penguin Masterstudies

This comprehensive list, designed to help advanced level and undergraduate studies, includes:

Subjects

Applied Mathematics
Biology
Drama: Text into Performance
Geography
Pure Mathematics

Literature

Dr Faustus
Eugenie Grandet
The Great Gatsby
The Mill on the Floss
A Passage to India
Persuasion
Portrait of a Lady
Tender Is the Night
Vanity Fair
The Waste Land

Chaucer

The Knight's Tale
The Miller's Tale
The Nun's Priest's Tale
The Pardoner's Tale
The Prologue to The Canterbury Tales
A Chaucer Handbook

Shakespeare

Hamlet
King Lear
Measure for Measure
Othello
The Tempest
A Shakespeare Handbook